Access 97
Basic Skills

Sue Coles

Department of Business and Management Studies
Crewe and Alsager Faculty
Manchester Metropolitan University

Jenny Rowley

School of Management and Social Sciences
Edge Hill University College

Letts
1997

Acknowledgments

This book would not have been completed without the support that the authors received, during its production, from many of their colleagues and family. They are particularly grateful to husbands Martyn and Peter, children Helen, Shula, Lynsey and Zeta, who had to make do with even less of their time than usual.

Windows 95™ and Access™ © Microsoft Corporation, all rights reserved. Screen displays from Access 97 and Windows 95 reprinted with permission from Microsoft Corporation.

A CIP record for this book is available from the British Library.

ISBN 1 85805 299 8

Reprinted 1998, 1999

Editorial and production services:Genesys Editorial

Typeset by Kai, Nottingham

Printed in Great Britain by Ashford Colour Press Ltd, Gosport, Hants.

Contents

About this book

Aims

This book is intended for students on a wide variety of business studies and other courses who need an introduction to databases through the use of Microsoft Access, one of the industry standard database packages. The book assumes no prior experience of a database package and concentrates on using Access at an introductory level. Progression beyond this level can be made by using *Access 97 Further Skills*.

Although this book is specifically designed for business studies students the orientation will be equally applicable to anyone wishing to learn the basics of using Access as well as to students in secondary, further, and higher education on many courses where familiarity with databases is required.

Structure

Anyone who has not used a Windows program before should first read through *Basic Windows Operations* (Unit 26) which summarises the key features of the Windows environment, and then turn to *Introduction to Access* (Unit 1). Those who are familiar with the Windows environment can move straight to *Introduction to Access* (Unit 1).

This book has 26 units.

To do this	Turn to...
Understand the basic concept of Access	Unit 1 Introduction to Access
Learn about tables, records and fields	Unit 2 Tables, records and fields
Create a new database	Unit 3 Creating a table in a new database
Define field properties	Unit 4 Defining field properties
Practise table design	Unit 5 Reviewing table design
Learn how to enter data	Unit 6 Entering and editing data
Delete, replace and print data	Unit 7 Managing, displaying and printing data
Practise data entry and management	Unit 8 Reviewing data entry and management
Select records using a filter	Unit 9 Using filters to select records
Question a database using a query	Unit 10 Introducing queries
Enter query criteria	Unit 11 Using query criteria
Practise sorting records and creating queries	Unit 12 Reviewing sorting and queries

Additional information

In Unit 25 you will find data required for some of the tasks in units throughout the book.

In Unit 26 you will find some basic information about Windows and definitions of buttons on all the Access toolbars.

What else do you need?

To carry out the activities in this book you will need a PC running Windows 95 and Access 97.

A note to lecturers and students

This book introduces students to the basics of databases through a series of application-oriented exercises. These exercises are based on the operations of one organisation, Chelmer Leisure and Recreation Centre. A series of self-contained but interrelated units takes the student through the design of a database for Chelmer Leisure and Recreation Centre. Each unit comprises a series of exercises. As each new function is introduced, the book explains both why the function is useful and how to use it.

As you progress through this book you will encounter a number of units whose titles commence with the term 'Reviewing'. Reviewing units are intended to give you an opportunity to check whether you have learnt the principles and skills embedded in the other units, and not simply followed instructions. Accordingly, reviewing units tell what to do, but not how to do it; they include very basic instructions, which if you have undergone the appropriate learning from the other units, you should be able to follow. Trainers or tutors may like to use these units to check learning progress. All the reviewing units are linked to each other, but are completely independent of the exercises in the remainder of the book. Thus, it is possible to complete either these units or the other units independently of one another. The reviewing units use a separate database, entitled Estates, which is a limited simulation of an estate agency database.

The approach does not assume any previous knowledge of databases or the Windows 95 environment. However, students who are familiar with the Windows 95 environment and, in particular, other Microsoft Office products such as Word, Excel and PowerPoint will find their road into Access to be much more intuitive than students who are not familiar with these related products. Equally, students who have some familiarity with other database products may find the database concepts introduced in this book easier to grasp.

The learning material requires little, if any, input by lecturers, and can therefore be used in programmes based on independent learning. Students learn by practising the commands and techniques.

This book may be used as a basis for independent study or for class activities. In either instance it is important to:

■ work methodically through the exercises in the order in which they are presented. Data entered in earlier exercises may be re-used in later exercises

■ take time for rest and reflection and break learning into manageable sessions

■ think about what you are doing

■ expect to make mistakes. Think about the consequences of any mistakes and learn from them

■ use the integrative exercises at the end of unit series as a means of testing whether you have understood the earlier concepts and exercises.

Lecturers' disk

A $3\frac{1}{2}''$ disk is available (free of charge to lecturers recommending the book as a course text) containing files of data for completing the exercises, plus the reports and queries produced via the exercises in the text. It can be used as a shortcut to avoid lengthy keying in of data and as a means of checking the outcomes of the exercises. The disk, or selected files from it, can be made available to students to allow them to check their own work.

Conventions

The following conventions have been adopted to distinguish between the various objects on the screen.

■ Dialog box names, menu items and commands are shown as **File-Print Preview**, which means choose the **File** menu and then select the option **Print Preview** from that menu; and **New Report**.

■ Buttons and icons are shown in bold inside shaded rectangles, e.g. **Design**

- Keys are shown in underlined italics, e.g. *Ctrl*

- Filenames, Table, form, query and report names are shown in bold, e.g. **Membership**

- Typed text is shown in bold italic, e.g. enter ***Smokers***

(d.) indicates text that gives a definition of a term. Note that all definitions are also included in the Glossary.

indicates a tip providing a helpful hint or short-cut method

(!) indicates a cautionary note.

indicates a cross reference.

Introduction to Access

What you will learn in this unit

This unit introduces the concept of a database and in particular a database created using Microsoft Access 97. At the end of this unit you should:

- understand the definition of a database

- be aware of the uses of databases, particularly in a business context

- be aware of the component parts of databases in general and Access in particular

- be aware of the Answer Wizard and Help facilities.

What you should already know

To use Access 97 you need to be familiar with Windows 95; it may be useful to refer to Unit 26 to refresh your memory.

What is a database?

A general definition of a database is that of being a *collection of related data* irrespective of the format of the data (written, electronic, audio, visual, etc). Today, the term database is often used to mean a collection of related data stored in a computer-readable format. Examples of collections of related data are employee details, stock details, medical histories.

When data is stored in a computer some software is needed to present that data to us, as users, in a form with which we can work. If we want to add to, edit or retrieve the data then the software must be able to translate our commands into a form the computer can use. This kind of software is known as a DataBase Management System (DBMS) and Access is one of the most powerful industry standard DBMSs that runs on a personal computer.

Task 1: Collections of data

In a collection of related data specific details are needed, for example, an estate agent keeping property details would need to know things such as: type of property, lease or freehold, selling price, address, number of rooms, description and size of rooms, heating, garage, garden, nearest schools, etc. There may also be other details so it is important to think about what they may be. For the following collections of data consider what specific details are needed:

- employee details

- students' academic histories

- stock in a sweet shop.

What are databases used for?

In large businesses databases are multi-user systems developed and maintained by Information Systems staff. However, many managers and staff, as well as small business owners are turning to smaller personal database management systems as a way to boost their productivity. In recent years the power of these has increased along with their ease of use, of which Access is a prime example.

In business, databases can be used by marketers to analyse customer preferences; sales managers to track sales and monitor the sales staff performance; accountants to keep records of business transactions. Data and information are an important resource for a business and a database management system provides the means to use this resource effectively.

Businesses used databases before computers were invented; a filing cabinet of customer details is a database, your personal address book is a database. The advantages that computer-based databases offer is the speed with which they work, the large quantities of data that they can handle and store in a relatively small space and their flexibility. There is a down-side: power-cuts, fire, flood, crime or terrorism can seriously threaten a business which relies on its electronic data, particularly if that business has not prepared itself for this kind of disaster.

What is an Access database?

 Access is a database management system and provides a means of storing and managing data or information. Microsoft refers to Access as a relational database product since it allows you to relate data from several different sets or tables. It is not the intention of this book to consider the relational aspect of database management systems. If, when you have finished this book, you would like to learn more then use the companion book in this series, *Access 97 Further Skills*.

There are four main components of an Access database, which will be considered at this introductory level. These are:

■ tables

■ queries

■ reports

■ screen forms.

Tables

Access stores data in tables that are organised by rows and columns. The basic requirement of having a database is that you have at least one table. The columns in the table represent specific details, for example, the selling price of a property. The rows contain the collection of specific details and are known as records. Records are discussed in more detail in the next unit.

Queries

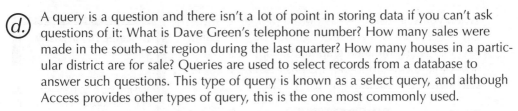

A query is a question and there isn't a lot of point in storing data if you can't ask questions of it: What is Dave Green's telephone number? How many sales were made in the south-east region during the last quarter? How many houses in a particular district are for sale? Queries are used to select records from a database to answer such questions. This type of query is known as a select query, and although Access provides other types of query, this is the one most commonly used.

Reports

Reports are used to print information. This may be based on all the data, in which case the report takes its input from a table, or it may be based on a selection of data, in which case the report takes its input from a query. Reports, therefore, can show the data from either a table or a query. In addition to data from records, they may show summary information relating to the data in the records displayed.

Screen forms

Screen forms are used to customise the way in which the data from records in tables or queries are displayed on screen. Their main purpose is to provide a user-friendly interface for the entry of new records or for editing existing records.

Text can be added to a form to act as labels and instructions to the person entering the data. The appearance of text on a form can be changed by changing the font or by adding bold or italic emphasis. Text can also be shown as raised or sunken or displayed in a specific colour, and lines and rectangles can be added to give the form a pleasing appearance.

Task 2: Components of databases

Answer the following questions:

1   What components of a database can a report be based upon?

2   What is a select query?

3   What is a table? Why is it the most important component of a database?

4   What is a screen form?

The Office Assistant

When you start using Access for the first time the Office Assistant will appear to guide you. The Office Assistant is an animated graphic that appears in a window of its own, and if your PC has a sound card, it also alerts your attention by using various sounds.

Clicking on the Office Assistant button in the toolbar controls whether or not the Office Assistant is displayed. When you have a question about how to do something you can ask the Office Assistant, for example, 'How do I create a query?' To do this click on the Assistant window and key your question into the **What would you like to do** box and click on the Search button.

The Assistant can, if you wish, provide help with tasks as you perform them without the need to ask questions.

You can choose an Assistant to match your personality, and as the Assistant is shared by the suite of Office programs, it will be a familiar guide when you are working with an application other than Access. To select a different Assistant, click on the Assistant button, click on Choose, click on the Gallery tab and choose one, but be prepared to install it from your Office 97 CD-ROM.

Welcome to Microsoft Access!

I'm the Office Assistant, and my job is to help you with this application.

- See key information for upgraders and new users
- Find out about the Office Assistant (That's me!)
- Start using Microsoft Access

A tour of the Access window and the Database window

It is worthwhile studying the two basic windows in Access - the Access window and the Database window - for a few moments before trying to make use of Access. This section can be used as a ready reference and returned to later as necessary.

The Access window

When you first start Access, by double-clicking on its icon and choosing **Start using Access**, the Access window shown in FIGURE 1.1 is displayed. Once you have used Access, on subsequent launches this window will appear. Here you may choose whether to create a new database or open an existing one. The background window is inactive but notice that it has the following components.

- **Title bar** - shows that you are in Microsoft Access.

- **Access** control menu - in the very top left hand corner.

- **Access** main menu - showing the menus.

- **Toolbar** – most icons are not available, as the **Microsoft Access** dialog box is active.

- **Status bar** – at the bottom of the screen. Indicates status, e.g. 'Ready'.

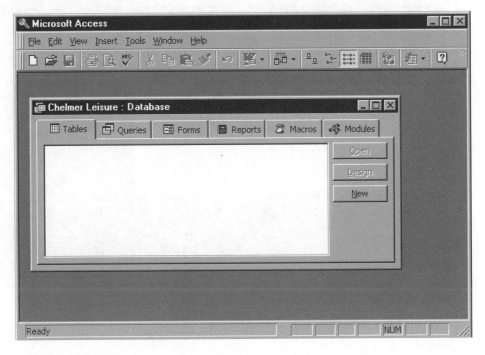

FIGURE 1.1: The Access window

The Database window

Once you have created (you will see how to do this in unit 3) or opened a database, a window like the one in FIGURE 1.2 is displayed. This window allows you to create or access any object (table, query, form, report, etc) in the database by clicking on one of the object 'tabs'. Initially the ▐ Tables ▐ tab is selected and a window displays all tables in the database. If the window is blank then none of that particular object has been created.

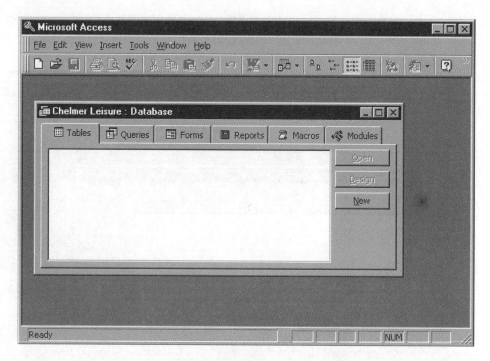

FIGURE 1.2 The Access window with the Database window displayed

When the Database window is open, the Access window has the following components.

- **Title bar**, which shows the Control menu icon (the key), the name of the application (i.e. Microsoft Access), and the window sizing buttons.

- **Database window main menu** showing the File, Edit, View, Insert, Tools, Window and Help pull-down menus.

- **Toolbar** which shows the icons for the creation of new objects. The icons vary depending on the object that you are working on. For example, when working on a table there are toolbar options for choosing a datasheet or design view. When designing a report, there are icons for previewing the report, and for sorting and grouping. All toolbar choices have equivalent menu selections.

- **Status bar**. Messages are displayed on the left of the status bar, for example, Ready. Modes are displayed on the right, for example, NUM indicates that the number section of the keyboard is in number rather than cursor control mode.

Help and the Office Assistant

Help is available through the Office Assistant, or by looking up an index of terms or by using the ' **What's this** ' pointer. There are four main methods of getting into the help system.

■ Pull down the **Help** menu and select **Microsoft Access Help**, press the function key *F1* or click on the `Office Assistant` button. The Office Assistant dialog box will pop-up with a choice of topics related to what you are currently doing as well a request box into which you can type a question.

■ Pull down the **Help** menu and select **Contents and Index**. The **Help Topics** dialog box appears. In this box there are three 'tabs' `Contents` , `Index` , and `Find` . Under the Contents section you may select any of the topics to find information about that topic. Under the Index section you may type in a word which is matched by the index about which you can display information. The Find section enables you to search for specific words and phrases in help topics, instead of searching by category or index.

■ Press *Shift+ F1* or pull down the Help menu and select **What's this**. The pointer changes to a pointer with a question mark (?) and it can be used to point to anything. Clicking on that object will then bring up help. For instance, in this way you may get help on the meaning of all of the items in the toolbar. To remove the question mark press *Esc*. Note that you must repeat this procedure if you want **Help** again this way.

■ Most dialog boxes have a help button on the title bar; it has a question mark (?) on it. Click on this and then click on the part of the dialog box which you want more information about.

Tables, records and fields

What you will learn in this unit

Before you create your database using Access you need to spend some time deciding what data are important to store and how you want Access to store them. You will create a table for storing the data. The table is composed of records, which are in turn composed of fields.

You will see that you need to consider the type of data for each field, for example, text or numeric. Even a fairly straightforward table of data will be easier to manage if it has been planned well.

By the end of this unit you will:

■ appreciate the reasons for analysing data before creating a database

■ understand that within a database data is kept in tables and that there may be more than one table in a database, which can be linked together

■ know that tables are composed of records which in turn are composed of fields

■ be aware of the different data types that are available with Access.

Database design

A database is used for storing data, and should be set up in such a way as to provide information to the person who originally stored the data. In large databases there are often more people involved in their design to meet particular needs, for example the database system used by a library or hospital. The designers are not usually the end-users and a lot of work goes into setting up such databases. It is not the intention of this book to impart design skills, rather to give you a practical insight into some of the basics through the building of simple databases.

In this unit we shall be considering the database needs of a small leisure centre, focusing on the data recorded about the members. Paralleling this as an integrative activity we shall consider the database needs of a small estate agent, focusing on the list of properties for sale. In a leisure centre or estate agency, data concerning other aspects of the business could be recorded, for example, details of rooms booked or prospective buyers' requirements. In Access this data could be recorded as additional tables in the database which could be linked together. However, this is beyond the scope of this book and you should proceed to the *Access 97 Further Skills* to discover more when you have completed this book.

A table generally holds data about one type of thing, for example, members (of the leisure centre) or properties (on an estate agent's books). There are usually lots of this particular thing, say, tens or hundreds of different members depending on the size of the leisure centre. A table of data about members of a leisure centre would hold details about each member.

Records and fields

A set of details about an individual member is known as a record. For each member there is a separate record in the table. Each record is composed of data about the member, such as name, address and so on. Each piece of data within the record is known as a field. As you progress through the units you will see how each field in a record needs to be defined before data can be entered into the record. Fields are given names to describe the kind of data they will eventually hold. It is important to distinguish between the name of a field and the data that that field contains. For example, the field named Lastname will hold people's last names such as Harris. The field names can be considered to be the column headings in the table and each row in the table is a separate record. Therefore each record in the table will have fields with the same name but containing different data.

It is important that each record is different from every other record so that it can be selected without confusion. If more than one person has the same last name the-some other field needs to be considered to differentiate between the records, for example, first name. An identifying field such as a number, say, employee number, is often created to make it easier to make each record unique. This field can be

used as a primary key - a field (or combination of fields) that uniquely identifies a record. We shall also see that fields need their size and the type of data that they will contain to be defined so that Access can store the data in the table correctly.

Choosing data types

The first stage in building the database is to define the table, that is, to give the table a name and define the names of the fields that will be contained in each record in the table.

The next stage is to define type of data to be stored in each of the fields. No data has yet been entered but before it can be, Access needs to know what sort of data to expect. Take the member's last name. First you need to tell Access the field name, i.e. Lastname, and you also need to tell Access whether the data is text, numeric, date/time etc before you can actually start entering people's names!

Every field in your table will be of a particular data type, for example a name is alphanumeric text, a price would be currency and a date would have a date data type. The data type that you choose for your field determines the kind and range of values that can be entered into it and the amount of storage space available in the field. Select the appropriate data type for each field. For example, you will probably define most fields in a table of names and addresses as Text fields.

There are likely to be instances where a Text field should be used when the data is numbers. Fields such as telephone numbers, or employee works numbers that contain only digits should be defined as Text fields. The reason for this is that there is no need to do calculations with telephone numbers or employee works numbers. Often telephone area codes start with a zero, which is not allowed in a true number.

Employee works numbers may also start with one or more zeros (known as leading zeros). So, reserve the Number data type for fields on which you want to perform calculations.

The following data types are available in Access:

- *Text*: Text and numbers. By default Access will make a text field 50 alphanumeric characters long, i.e. you can enter up to 50 letters and numbers. If you know the length of the longest piece of data to be entered into the field then you can specify this as anything from 1 to 255 characters. Examples of text type fields: names and addresses, class activity.

- *Number*: Numerical data on which you intend to perform mathematical calculations, except calculations involving money. You will see later that there are different Number data types that you can choose, which define the size of number you wish to store and whether the data is whole numbers or decimal numbers. Example of numeric field: number of items in stock.

- *Auto Number*: Sequential whole numbers automatically inserted by Microsoft Access so you don't need to enter the data into the field. Numbering begins with one and increments by one each time data for a new record is entered. Makes a good primary key field as each number is unique for each record, however, as a consequence you cannot edit this number and if you later delete a record that number is 'lost'. This data type is used primarily to give uniqueness to each record, for example, a membership number or a product identification number.

- *Date/Time*: Dates and times. A variety of display formats are available, or you can create your own. Example: date of joining.

- *Currency*: Money. Don't use the Number data type for currency values because numbers to the right of the decimal may be rounded during calculations. The Currency data type maintains a fixed number of digits to the right of the decimal. Example: membership fee.

- *Yes/No*: Yes/No, True/False, On/Off. Example: smoker/non-smoker.

- *Memo*: Lengthy text and numbers. A Memo field can contain up to 32,000 characters. For example, comments about a hotel in a travel company's database.

Task 1: Data types

Think about the following questions:

1 What would be the effect of rounding on currency (money) data?

2 What data type do you think you would choose for the following fields?

- Category No

- Lastname

- Street

- Telephone No

■ Date of Birth

■ Sporting Interests

3 Later you will find that we use a Yes/No field for Sex. Explain this!

4 Why would you use a text field for a postcode?

Task 2: Choosing data types

Consider creating a table listing properties held in a small estate agent's database. What fields would you choose for each record and what field names would you give them? Which data types would you use? What field or combination of fields would make each record in such a table different from every other record?

 This table will be set up in Unit 5 and you will able to review your choice of fields with those chosen by the authors.

Creating a table in a new database

What you will learn in this unit

This unit focuses on the creation of a database table in an Access database file. A database file is used to store all the components of an Access database, which you will be creating as you work through these units.

The creation of a table requires the definition of the fields in the table. Each field requires a name to distinguish it from the other fields and the type of data which is to be stored in the field needs to be defined.

By the end of this unit you will be able to:

■ define a new database

■ retrieve this database

■ recognise component parts of a table

■ create a table

■ define data types for fields.

Creating a database

A new database is used to store the table, and all queries, forms and reports that are needed to provide information from the table. To begin with our database will hold the table of data needed for the leisure centre example.

Task 1: Defining a new database

1   Start Access by double clicking on its icon. Choose the Create a New Database Using Blank Database option and press the **OK** button.

2   In the New Database dialog box select the drive and directory in which you wish to store your database. | If you do not change directory then your database is likely to be stored in the **My Documents** folder provided by Windows 95.

3   In the **File Name** box type in the filename ***Chelmer Leisure***. obeying the
filename rules opposite.

Access will give it the extension of .mdb.
This file differs from traditional PC databases in that it can contain all of the
tables, forms, reports, queries, etc that
belong to a database. Access, as it is running in the Windows 95 environment,
allows you to use long descriptive filenames.

The complete path to the file including
drive letter, folder path name and filename can contain up to 255 characters.
Any characters may be used except the
following: * ? ; \ / : " | < >. You cannot
use a period (full stop) except to separate
the filename from the extension.

4   Click on **Create**.

Note that Access stores all tables, forms,
queries, reports etc in this one file. The
file you have just created awaits the
inclusion of these as you learn to create
them.

Closing and opening a database

When you have finished working with the database you can close the database
using **File-Close**. If you have made changes which you haven't saved, then Access
will prompt you to save them.

To open an existing database use **File-Open Database** or click on the
Open Database button in the toolbar. Select the drive and directory in which
your database is stored and select the file name and click on **Open**.

When you have finished working with Access you can close the application using
File-Exit. Next time you start Access you will see your database listed in the **Open
an existing database** section of the **Microsoft Access** dialog box. Simply click on it
to open the database.

Task 2: Closing and opening the Chelmer database

Although we have not created a table as yet, the database file exists and this task
will show you how to close it and then open it again. You will do this many times
in the course of these units.

1   To close the database, choose **File-Close**.

2   To open the database, choose **File-Open Database**. In the **Open** dialog box
select the drive and directory in which your database is stored.

3   Select the file **Chelmer Leisure** from the list below the **Look in** box.

4   Click on ▮ **Open** ▮.

5   To close Access, choose **File-Exit**.

6   To open Access and choose an existing database. Start Access by clicking on its icon.

7   Select the file **Chelmer Leisure** from the list in the **Open an existing database** section. Click ▮ **OK** ▮.

Defining a new table

This section takes the form of a series of tasks in which the **Membership** table will be defined. You will set up the fields so that they correspond to the type of data that will be stored in those fields.

Task 3: Creating a new table

1 Check the database window is still active.	It should still be open after the last task. It is indicated by a blue title bar if you are using the standard Windows colours.

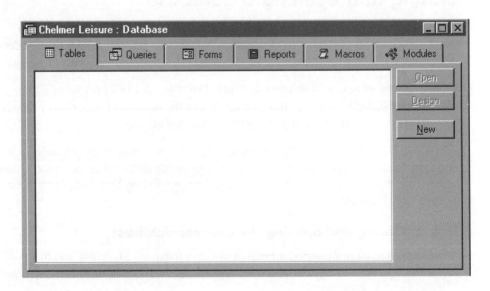

FIGURE 3.1

2   If the ▮ **Tables** ▮ tab is not selected as shown in the illustration then click on it.

3   Click on the ▩New▩ button in the table window to display the New Table dia-
    log box

FIGURE 3.2

4   Select Design View and click on the ▩OK▩ button to display the Table Design
    window.

(d.) The Table Design window (FIGURE 3.3) allows you to define the structure of your
table. By filling in the Field Name, Data Type and Description cells and by setting
Field Properties the structure of the table is defined. This is described in the following task.

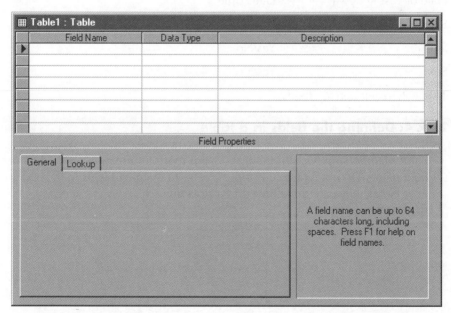

FIGURE 3.3 Table Design window

In the next task you will define the fields for the **Membership** table and enter the name, data type and description into the Table Design window.

Field Name	Data Type	Description
Membership No	AutoNumber	Automatic membership numbering
Category No	Number	Categories are 1-Senior, 2-Senior Club, 3-Junior, 4-Junior Club, 5-Concessionary, 6-Youth Club
Lastname	Text	
Firstname	Text	
Title	Text	
Street	Text	
Town	Text	
County	Text	
Post Code	Text	
Telephone No	Text	
Occupation	Text	
Date of Birth	Date/Time	
Date of Joining	Date/Time	
Date of Last Renewal	Date/Time	
Sporting Interests	Memo	
Smoker	Yes/No	
Sex	Yes/No	

TABLE 3.1 Membership fields

Task 4: Defining the fields in a table

1 Enter **Membership No.** for the first field name. Do not type a full stop after No as these are not allowed in field names.

For more information on field names refer to Naming Fields in the text later in this unit.

2 Press *Enter* to move to the Data Type column and click on the down arrow button which displays the Data Type list box.

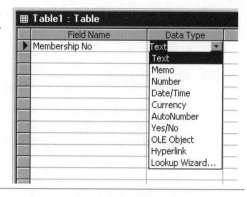

3 Click on the data type AutoNumber. Press *Enter* and you will be in the description field. Key in the description as shown in Table 3.1. Press *Enter* to move to the next field.

See later in the unit for details of moving around the Table Design window.

4 Continue to enter the definitions for the fields as detailed in the table. Where there is no description press *Enter* to take you to the next field.

The table will be revisited later to set individual field properties.

5 The next stage is to define the primary key. Click on the row selector (see later in the unit) for Membership No and click on the **Primary Key** button in the tool bar.

Primary Keys will be discussed in more detail later.

Move on to the next task to save this table definition.

Saving the table definition

Once the structure of the table has been designed it needs to be saved. Access uses this information to set up templates through which you enter data into the table.

The table is saved as part of the database file and its name distinguishes it from other tables in the database file. There may be more than one table in a database file and Access allows freedom for naming tables. You will also find this true for naming queries, forms, reports and macros as all these are stored in one database file. Make use of this freedom to give meaningful names to tables as they will be used later in queries, forms and reports and it is important to be able to recognise the name of the table you require.

Task 5: saving the table definition

Continuing from the previous task:

1   Choose **File-Save**.

2   In the **Save As** dialog box, in the   Note that the name that you choose may
    Table Name box type the name   be 255 characters long and contain any
    Membership. Click the OK button.   alphanumeric text.

3   Close the table using **File-Close**.   Shortcut key *Ctrl-W*

Closing and opening the table

To close a table, either double-click on the table's control menu button, or choose
File-Close. ▣

You can open an existing table in either Design View or Datasheet view. So far we
have only considered the Design View of a table.

To open a table in Design View

1   In the Database window, click on the Tables tab.

2   Select the table you want to open, and then click on the Design button.

In the next task you will open the **Membership** table in Design View.

Task 6: Opening a table

In this task the **Membership** table will be opened in Design View:

1   In the Database window, click on the Tables tab.

2   Select the table **Membership**.

3   Click on the Design button.

Moving around the table design window

Through the table design window you can enter the field name, the data type and a
description of each field (the description is optional) into the grid in the upper part
of the window. To move between cells you have a choice of pressing either *Enter*,
Tab , ➔ or clicking in the required cell in the grid.

Row selector symbols

Along the left hand edge of the grid you will see the row selector symbols. By clicking in the row selector box you can select an entire row.

Row	*Selector symbol*
Current row	▶
Primary key field	🔑

Naming fields

Fields need names, lengths and data types to be defined. Many database products limit you to about 10 characters for a field name, which means that they often need to be abbreviated. Spaces in a field name are not usually allowed in other products. Access allows field names to be up to 64 characters long with spaces. Field names should be meaningful so that the data is easier to work with. Some characters are not allowed in field names:

■ full stops (.)

■ exclamation marks (!)

■ square brackets ([]).

You cannot give the same name to more than one field. Why not?

The length of a field may be pre-determined according to the data type of that particular field. If the field is of a date type then it will have a standard length. Other data types such as text and number can have their lengths defined. If a text field is being used to hold the title of a song, for example, then you need to estimate the length of the longest song title and set the size of the field accordingly.

Adding field description

A description for a field may be added into the description cell in the table's Design View, for any field. The maximum length for the description is 255 characters. It is not necessary to enter a description but it can be useful to provide additional information about a particular field.

Correcting mistakes in field name or description

Point and click in the cell containing the mistake. Correct the mistake in a normal fashion by inserting or deleting text at the insertion point. Click back in the current cell to continue working.

Correcting mistakes in the data type

Click on the data type cell concerned. Open the list box and select the correct data type.

Creating a primary key

The primary key is a field or combination of fields that uniquely identifies each record in a table. Though not required, a primary key is highly recommended. It speeds data retrieval and if you move on to using more than one table in your database, it enables you to define default relationships between tables. In the membership table the membership number is the primary key; each record has a different number, as every member's number will be different.

If the table does not include an obvious primary key field, you can have Microsoft Access set up a field that assigns a unique number to each record. This automatically numbers each record uniquely.

Setting or changing the primary key

To set or change the primary key,

1 In the table's Design View, select the field or fields you want to define as the primary key. To select one field, click the row selector. To select multiple fields, hold down the Ctrl key, and click the row selectors for each field.

2 Click on the **Primary Key** button on the tool bar, or choose **Edit-Primary Key**. Microsoft Access places the primary key icon in the row selector column.

To have Access define the primary key.

1 With the table's Design View displayed, save the table without specifying a primary key. Access asks if you want it to create a primary key field.

2 Choose **Yes** and Access creates a field in your table called ID with the AutoNumber data type.

Defining field properties

What you will learn in this unit

Once a database table has been created and the fields named and the type of data which is to be stored in the field chosen, you can make further refinements to fields by setting field properties. It is important to maintain documentation concerning the fields and the properties chosen for them. A standard way to do this is by printing a table definition using Access' Documenter facility.

By the end of this unit you will be able to:

- define field properties

- create data validation rules

- select custom display formats

- print out the field properties (table design).

Defining field properties

(d.) You may have noticed that once you start to enter the field definitions, field name, data type and description, then the field properties are displayed in the lower left hand section of the Design window (FIGURE 4.1). You have defined the basic data type for each field and by setting the field properties you can specify the data type in more detail, for example, if the data type is text you can define the length of the field.

General	Lookup
Field Size	10
Format	
Input Mask	
Caption	
Default Value	
Validation Rule	
Validation Text	
Required	No
Allow Zero Length	No
Indexed	No

FIGURE 4.1 Field properties

In the Field Properties section, you can set properties for individual fields. The available options depend on the data type you define for the field. In the lower right hand section of the window a description of the current column or field property is displayed.

Each field has a set of properties you use to specify how you want data stored, handled, and displayed. You set the properties in the bottom part of the Table window's Design View. The properties you can set for each field are determined by the data type you select for the field.

Setting a field property

1   In the table's Design View, select the field whose properties you want to set.

2   Click the property you want to set in the bottom part of the window.

3   Set the property, as explained in the following table.

Property	Description
Field Size	Maximum length of the text field or type of Number
Format	How data is displayed; use predefined formats or customise your own
Input Mask	Data entry pattern
Caption	Default field label in a form or report
Default Value	Value entered in a field when records are created
Validation Rule	Expression that defines data entry rules
Validation Text	Text for invalid data
Required	Whether or not an entry must be made
Allow Zero Length	Allows you to store a zero length string ("") to indicate data that exists but is unknown.
Indexed	Single-field indexes to speed searches

Field size

This property sets the maximum size of data that can be stored in a field. If the Data Type property is set to Text, enter a number less than 255. You should choose this number by considering the length of the longest text data that is to be entered into the field. The default setting is 50.

If the Data Type property is set to Number, the Field Size property settings and their values are related in the following way.

Setting	Description
Byte	Stores whole numbers with values between 0 to 255. Occupies 1 byte.
Integer	Stores whole numbers with values between –32,768 and 32,767. Occupies 2 bytes.
Long Integer	Stores numbers from –2,147,483,648 to 2,147,483,647 (no fractions). Occupies 4 bytes.
Single	Stores numbers with six digits of precision, from –3.402823E38 to 3.402823E38. Occupies 4 bytes.
Double (Default)	Stores numbers with ten digits of precision, from –1.79769313486232E308 to 1.79769313486232E308. Occupies 8 bytes.

Defaults

Access will assign default values to the fields in your table. This default value is automatically entered in the field when a new record is created. These are values that are usually appropriate for the addition of new records to a table. The default value for **Number**, **Currency** and **Yes/No** fields is zero, in the case of **Yes/No** fields zero means No. **Text**, **Memo** and **Date** fields are empty by default. You can save time by specifying your own default values for fields.

You can specify a default field using text or an expression. For example, in an address table you might set the default for the Town field to London, if the majority of records are London addresses. When users add records to the table, they can either accept this value or enter the name of a different town or city. If, for example, an Orders table contains the field Order Date then the expression =Date() can be used to put the current date into this field.

Validation

The data entered into tables must be accurate if the database is to be valuable to the person or organisation that it serves. However, even the most experienced data entry operators can make mistakes. To try to detect mistakes you can test the data entered by creating validation rules. These are simple tests, which are entered as short expressions into the **Validation Rule** text box.

If the data entered does not conform to your validation rule, a message box will be displayed to inform the operator that the data is incorrect. The message in the message box is defined by the text that you put in the Validation Text text box. The maximum length for both the Validation Rule and the Validation Text boxes is 255 characters. If data in a record is amended then the validation will still be performed. If a validation rule for a field hasn't been entered then no validation will be performed on that field.

Examples of expressions that can be used are often concerned with numeric fields, e.g. a credit limit that cannot be greater than a certain value. Fields with other data types may also be validated, for example a date may only be entered in a certain

23

time period, or a department code can be checked to see if it is a correct department code.

Required entry

If you set the required property of a field to Yes you will need to make an entry in
that particular field for every record. Where it is not necessary to have an entry this
property can be left as its default value. In the **Membership** table the **Category No**
field has been defined as a required field. A member cannot be enrolled without
being given a category of membership. As you create the **Membership** table in the
next task, consider which fields in this table are required entry and set this property.

Task 1: Defining field properties

So far we have not changed any of the field properties. In this task you will define
the field properties of the **Membership** table. You should be able to complete this
task by following the immediate instructions, but additional notes are also given in
the following few pages, which you may wish to consult.

1   From the **Database** window with the **Tables** tab selected click on
    Membership and click on the **Design** button.

2   Select the field **Category No**.   This field has a data type of Number and
                                                     the Field Properties are preset as Field
                                                     Size - Double, Decimal Places - Auto,
                                                     Default Value – 0, Required – No and
                                                     Indexed - No. In this field the data that
                                                     will be entered is a number between 1
                                                     and 6 inclusive, as there are 6 cate-
                                                     gories. Refer back to the section entitled
                                                     Field size to see a list of the different
                                                     number properties that are available. The
                                                     Byte number type allows whole numbers
                                                     up to 255 so is a good choice for the
                                                     number property of the **Category No**
                                                     field.

3   Click in the **Field Size** box, open its   There are only six categories so a valida-
    associated list and select Byte.   tion rule can be created.

4   Click in the Validation Rule box and key in **<=6** and key in the text ***Please enter
    a category number between 1 and 6*** into the **Validation Text** box.

5   Open the **Required** list box and select **Yes**. It is necessary for there to be an entry
    in this field.

6   Select the field **Lastname**.

7   Click in the Field Size box, delete the default size of 50 and replace it with **25**.

8   Alter the sizes of the other text fields as follows:

■ **Firstname**   **30**

■ **Title**   **10**

■ **Street**   **30**

■ **Town**   **25**

■ **County**   **20**

■ **Post Code**   **10**

■ **Telephone No**   **12**

9   Select the **Town** field again and in the Default Value box type **Chelmer**.

10 Select the **County** field and put   Why do think these defaults are set?
    Cheshire into its Default Value box.   (Refer to the section on defaults earlier in
                                              this unit.)

11 Select the **Date of Birth** field and in the Format box key the format d/m/yy (to
    suppress leading zeros on day and month) or dd/mm/yy (to display leading
    zeros). Repeat this for the two other date fields. Alternatively, select Short Date
    from the drop down list of the Format box.

12 Select the **Smoker** field and in the   Note it is important to put the first semi-
    Format box replace Yes/No with the   colon.
    format **;"Smoker";"Non-smoker"**
    which will display Smoker for Yes
    and Non-Smoker for No.

13 Click on the Lookup tab then click   This is so the defined formats will be dis-
    on the down arrow of the Display   played.
    Control drop down list box. Select
    Text box. Click on the General
    tab.

14 Select the **Sex** field and in the Format box replace Yes/No with the format
    10;"Male;'Female; which will display Male for Yes and Female for No. Set the
    display control to text box as for the **Smoker** field.

15 Save the changes using File-Save and close the table using File-Close.

Creating custom display formats

Custom formats will display the data in the format that is specified regardless of the format in which it is entered. For example a display format can be created which will show all telephone numbers using a particular format e.g. (01777) 565656 or 01777-565656. A custom format is created from an image of the format. To design the image a special set of characters, known as placeholders are used. To illustrate the creation of a custom format some examples are shown in the following table.

Format	*Example*
Numeric format	The # indicates the place for a digit but if the place is not used then leading and trailing zeros are not shown. The 0 indicates a place for a digit and if the place is not used then a 0 is shown. The comma may be used as a thousands separator.
##,###.00	56.98 6.90 5,890.07 100.00
#0.000	12.456 0.020
Date	The days placeholder is d. d displays 1, dd 01, ddd Mon, dddd Monday. The months placeholder is m. m displays 1, mm 01, mmm Jan, mmmm January. The years placeholder is y. yy displays 96, yyyy 1996. The / or - separates the day, month and year.
dddd d mmmm yyyy	Tuesday 26 March 1996
dd/mm/yy	26/06/96
d-m-yy	2-5-94 (this format does not display leading zeros).
Time	The hours placeholder is h. h displays 3, hh 03. The minutes placeholder is m. m displays 6, mm 06. The seconds placeholder is s. s displays 7, ss 07. The colon separates hours, minutes and seconds. AM/PM or am/pm displays time in 12 instead of 24-hour format.
h:mm AM/PM	6:34 PM
hh:mm:ss	11:09:57
Text	@ indicates that a character is required in the partic-ular position.
>	Changes all text in the field to uppercase.
<	Changes all text in the field to lowercase.
(@@@@@) @@@@@@	(01777) 565656
Yes/No	;"Male";"Female" Displays Male for true and Female for false.

Task 2: Custom display format

1 Open the **Chelmer Leisure** database and open the **Membership** table in Design View.

2 Select the **Post Code** field and type **>** in the **Format** property box.

3 Save and close the table using **File-Save** followed by **File-Close**.

Making a printed copy of the table design

Access allows you to view and print the design characteristics (definition) of your tables, forms, queries and reports. To make a printed copy of the table design

1 Choose **Tools-Analyze**, and then click **Documenter**. Note: you may need to install Access' analysing tools.

2 Click on the **Tables** tab.

3 Click on the name of the table for which definitions are required and click on **Select**.

4 Click **Options** to specify which features of the selected object you want to print, and then click on **OK**.

5 Click **OK** in the Documenter window.

6 You might want to check the length of your definitions in the Print Preview window, because some definitions, particularly those for forms and reports, can be many pages long.

7 To print the definition, click on the **Print** button in the toolbar.

Before such tools were available, database designers created another table as a means of storing table definitions, i.e. a data dictionary. This required more work but gave a more complete perspective and a chance to revise the work already done. Each data element in the database system had an entry in a dictionary table.

Task 3: Printing the Membership table definition

1 Display the Database window, and follow steps 1 to 3, above. Choose the **Membership** table and click on **Options**.

2 Set the following options
   ■ Include for Table: Properties
   ■ Include for Fields: Names, Data types and Size
   ■ Include for Indexes: Nothing

3   Click on   OK .

4   Click on   OK   in the Documenter window. You will be prompted to close the table. Click   Yes . Be prepared that Access may take a little time to compile the definition.

5   Preview and print the table definition.

Creating another table in a database

Access is a relational database and allows more than one table in a database to be created. There is usually a link between tables but this is not necessary. As this is an introductory text, relationships between tables will not be considered so the new table that is to be added to the Chelmer Leisure database is one which involves the centre but does not directly link to the Membership table. It is included since it is a small table and tasks based upon it in future units are simpler in nature. It also illustrates how an Access database can hold a collection of tables and it serves to practise table creation techniques.

Task 4: Creating the Classes table

The **Classes** table is a second table in the **Chelmer Leisure** database.

1   Open the **Chelmer Leisure** database.

2   Choose to create a new table in Design View.

3   Define the structure of the basic table with reference to the following information and define **Class No** as the primary key:

Field Name	Data Type	Description
Class No	AutoNumber	
Class Day	Text	
Class Time	Date/Time	
Class Tutor	Text	
Class Activity	Text	
Male/Female/Mixed	Text	

4   Set the field properties as indicated below

Field	Property	Setting
Class Day	Field Size	10
	Required	Yes
Class Time	Format	Short Time (equivalent to hh:mm)
	Required	Yes
Class Tutor	Field Size	30
Class Activity	Field Size	20
	Required	Yes
Male/Female/Mixed	Field Size	10
	Validation Rule	"Male" or "Female" or "Mixed"
	Validation Text	Please enter Male Female or Mixed

5   Save and close the table **Classes.** Print the table design using the same options as for the previous task and close the table. Data will be entered into this table via a screen form, which you will create in Unit 13.

6   Close the **Chelmer Leisure** database.

Reviewing table design

What you will learn in this unit

This is the first Reviewing Unit as mentioned in the introduction to this book. Here you have an opportunity to check whether you have learnt the principles and skills embedded in Units 1 to 4, and not simply followed instructions. Accordingly, this unit will tell you what to do but not how to do it. Only very basic instructions are given, which, if you have undergone the appropriate learning from the other units, you should be able to follow. This unit reviews and offers further practice on the following topics:

■ creating a database and designing a table

■ defining field properties.

The series of Reviewing Units uses a separate database, entitled Chelmer Estates, which is a limited simulation of an estate agency database.

Task 1: Creating the Chelmer Estates database and its main table, called Properties

This task introduces the database that will be used throughout the Reviewing Units in this book, **Chelmer Estates**, and its main table **Properties**.

1   Create a new database called **Chelmer Estates**

2   Create a new table in the **Chelmer Estates** database, called **Properties**, which is to include the following fields:

Field Name	Data Type	Description
Property No	AutoNumber	automatic registration numbering
Address	Text	number, street name
Town	Text	
House Type	Number	1=bungalow, 2=detached, 3=semi-detached, 4=terraced, 5=flat
Number of Bedrooms	Number	
Garage	Number	1=single, 2=double, 3=none
Garden Length	Number	
Leasehold/Freehold	Yes/No	
Selling Price	Currency	
Heating	Number	1=gas, 2=electric, 3=solid fuel, 4=oil
Date of Entry	Date/Time	
Notes	Memo	

FIGURE 5.1

3   Save the table definition as **Properties**.

Access displays a message asking if you want to create a primary key. Click on No . If you wish to set a primary key choose **Property No.**

Task 2: Defining field properties

1   If necessary, open the **Properties** table.

2   Set the field length of the text fields thus:

■ **Address:** *30*

■ **Town:** *25*

3   Select the **Town** field and enter Default Value of *Chelmer*.

4   Create validation rules for the **House Type**, **Garage** and **Heating** fields, which prevent numbers higher than the valid numbers for their respective categories being entered. Also create corresponding validation messages in the Validation Text property.

5   Select the **Leasehold/Freehold** field and set the format to *;"Leasehold";"Freehold"* instead of Yes/No (note: remember that the initial ; is important)

6   Select a date format for the **Date of Entry** field (suggest Long Date).

7   Save the table definition again and print the **Properties** table definition using the options set for the **Membership** table in the Chelmer Leisure database.

Columns

Name	Type	Size	
Property No	Number (Long)	4	
Address	Text	30	
Town	Text	25	
House Type	Number (Long)	4	
Number of Bedrooms	Number (Long)	4	
Garage	Number (Long)	4	
Garden Length	Number (Long)	4	
Leasehold/Freehold	Yes/No	1	
Selling Price	Currency	8	
Heating	Number (Long)	4	
Date of Entry	Date/Time	8	
Notes	Memo	-	

FIGURE 5.2

To print a more comprehensive table definition, choose the Names, Data types, Sizes and Properties option for fields in the Documenter, but note that this will be nearly four pages long as all field properties are listed.

8   Close the **Chelmer Estates** database.

Entering and editing data

What you will learn in this unit

By the end of this unit you will be able to:

■ display a table's datasheet and use it to enter data

■ navigate around the datasheet so that data can be edited.

Entering data

The next stage is to enter data into the tables. Up until now the table has only been opened in Design View. To enter data a table needs to be opened in the Datasheet View.

1   In the Database window, if the **Table** tab is not selected then click on it.

2   Double-click the table name, or select the table and choose the **Open** button. The table will open in Datasheet View.

Once a table is open it is possible to switch from the Datasheet view to the Design View and vice versa. If you make changes to the design you will be asked to save them if you switch back to the Datasheet View. There is a button on the tool bar for switching between the views:

When in Design View	When in Datasheet View

Datasheet View button   Design View button

In the Datasheet view the headings of the columns are the field names you designed previously. Each row in the datasheet is a record and as you complete each record it is automatically saved into the table.

Task 1: Membership data

1   Open the **Chelmer Leisure** database and open the **Membership** table in Datasheet view.

Notice that there are some fields already filled in these are the default values. A default value can be accepted or it can be overridden.

2 Do not enter a value into the membership number field but press *Enter* to move to the next field.

This is a counter field and if you do try to enter data into it the entry will not be accepted. When you press Enter after entering data into the last field of the first record, Access saves the record. Notice what appears in the membership number field. Let Access number all the membership number fields.

3. Enter the data for the **Membership** table as shown in Unit 25. After entering the data for each field move to the next by pressing *Enter, Tab* or ➜. When entering the data for the logical fields enter either **Yes** or **No** and the appropriate word as defined by the format appears, e.g. Male or Female.

Also while entering the data test the validation rules, those that Access applies and those that have been defined. Try the following:

■ enter text into a date-type field, Access expects the correct data type, and the Office Assistant will inform you of your mistake (see illustration),

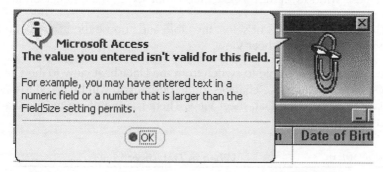

■ enter a Category No greater than 6; this will test the validation rule set up in the field properties for Category No.

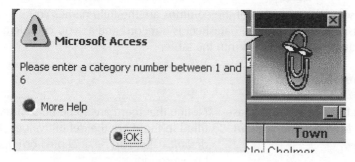

Skip fields that are blank. Validation, skipping fields and using Undo are described below.

Validation

Data is validated as it is entered, if it does not conform to the data type set for that field an error message will be generated. If the data entered breaks the validation rule that has been set as a property for that field, then if there is validation text, this appears as the error message.

Skipping fields, null values

Sometimes not all the data for a record is available, for example, the telephone number may be missing. To skip a field, simply press *Enter* or *Tab* to take you to the next field. It is acceptable to skip fields where the data is not vital but for data such as the Membership No it is not acceptable. Access automatically enters a membership number as the field was defined with a Counter data type.

 Where a field is left without an entry it is said to be Null, i.e. there is nothing there. If you perform mathematical calculations on numeric fields, then Access ignores fields containing Nulls.

Using Undo

Should you do anything wrong or if something unexpected happens always try **Edit-Undo** or click on the ▉ **Undo** ▉ button before doing anything else.

Editing data

Once you have entered the records into a table, this data is available to be used, as is evident in the following sessions. However, you can view the data in the datasheet and if you spot mistakes you can rectify them.

Moving between records

By using either **Edit-Go To**, the *Up* and *Down Arrow* keys, *Page Up* and *Page Down* keys, or the vertical scroll bar you can move between records in the datasheet. However, the most efficient way to move between records in large databases is with the navigation buttons in the lower-left corner of the window.

Access record indicators

In the status bar of the datasheet window are the Access record indicators. These are record movement buttons and the record number of the currently selected record.

To move to	Click
First record	⏮
Last record	⏭
Previous record	◀
Next record	◀
New record	▶*

Specific record click in record counter box [_____1]

(or press *F5*), type the record number you want, and then press *Enter*.

Selecting data

Various parts of the datasheet can be selected; when an area is selected it appears in inverse colour, so if text is normally black on white, then selected text is white on black.

To select	Do this
A single field	Move the pointer to the left-hand side of a cell, so that it changes shape into a white cross and click.
A word in a field	Double-click on the word.
A record	Click in the record selector at the left edge of the record, or choose **Edit-Select Record**.
More than one record	Click and drag in the record selector edge for the required number of records.
A field column	Click on the column heading (the field name at the top of the column).
Several field columns	Click on the first column heading required for the selection and drag to the last.

Moving and copying fields

You can move a field by selecting it, using **Edit-Cut**, clicking in the cell where the field is to be moved to and using **Edit-Paste**.

You can copy a field by selecting it, using **Edit-Copy**, clicking in the cell where the copy is required and using **Edit-Paste**. Buttons are available, i.e. **Cut**, **Copy** and

Paste .

Hiding and showing columns

If there are a lot of fields in a table as is the case with the **Membership** table then columns may be hidden. By using the Show command the columns may be redisplayed. To hide a column in a datasheet:

1   click on the column selector at the top of the column; more than one column may be selected for hiding;

2   choose **Format-Hide Columns**.

To redisplay the columns:

1   choose **Format-Unhide Columns**

2   in the dialog box select the column(s) to be unhidden and click on Close .

Managing data

What you will learn in this unit

By the end of this unit you will be able to:

■ delete data

■ use find and replace to edit data

■ print the data in your table.

Deleting records

 You can delete a record from a table using a datasheet or a form. (You will meet forms in Unit 13.) Here you see how to delete records using a datasheet.

To delete a record.

1   Select the record or records you wish to delete.

2   Press the *Delete* key (or choose **Edit-Delete** from the menu).

3   Access prompts you to confirm the deletion. Choose **OK** to delete the record or **Cancel** to restore it.

Finding and replacing

To find a particular field.

1   If you wish to find a particular entry in a certain field make that field current by clicking in that column.

2   Choose either **Edit-Find** or click on the **Find** button in the toolbar. Key the string (set of characters) you wish to find into the **Find What** text box.

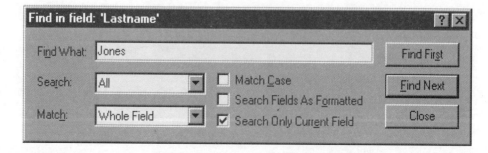

3   In the Search: box choose between Up, Down or All.

4   In the Match: box select whether your string should match the whole field, any part of the field or the start of the field. A string is a collection of characters (letters, numbers, and punctuation marks) making up the data element in a field, e.g. a word or telephone number.

5   In the Match Case tick box you may choose between making your search case sensitive or not. (A case sensitive search exactly matches the case (upper or lower) as defined in the Find What box.)

6   In the Search Fields As Formatted tick box you may choose between finding a field as say, a number 28/3/96 or as it is formatted 28-Mar-96.

7   Using the Search Only Current Field tick box you may choose between limiting your search to the current field or including all fields.

8   To start the search click on either **Find Next** , which will search from your current position in the direction you have chosen, or **Find First** which will find the first occurrence in the field or table.

9   Each time a match is found it is highlighted. If either the top or the bottom of the table is reached Access displays a message saying that it has finished searching the records.

10 When you have found the desired field click on **Close** .

To replace a particular field, select Edit-Replace and the steps are the same as for finding a field, except that in the dialog box there is an additional text box, Replace With, into which the replacement string is entered. Strings can be replaced according to which button is clicked.

Button	Action
Find Next	Finds and highlights but does not replace. Use when you don't want to replace.
Replace	Replaces the highlighted string and finds the next occurrence of the Find What string.
Replace All	Replaces all occurrences of the string without stopping.
Close	Closes the dialog box.

Task 1: Editing data

In this task we experiment with finding and replacing data.

1   Open the **Membership** table. Move to the end of the table.

2 Add another record, Category 3. Move to record 9, select the Lastname field and copy it, using Edit-Copy.

3 Move back to the **Lastname** field of the new record and use **Edit-Paste**. Finish the record as shown in the table below:

Firstname	Title	Street	Town	County	Post Code
Frances	Miss	70 Meir View	Chelmer	Cheshire	CH2 7BZ

Date of Birth	Date of Joining	Date of Last Renewal	Sporting interests	Smoker	Sex
5/5/82	1/3/95	1/3/96	Swimming, Judo	No	No

4 Go to the first record. Click in the **Telephone No** field.

5 Choose **Edit-Find** or click on the **Find** button in the toolbar.

6 Key **01778** into the **Find What** box and select **Start of field** in the **Match** box.

7 Click on the **Find First** button.   This should highlight the first occurrence. If the **Find in field** dialog box is in the way drag it out of the way.

8 Click on the **Find Next** button to find other matches. Close the **Find in field** dialog box.

9 Move to the top of the table again and click in the **Telephone No** field. Choose **Edit-Replace** and key **01777** into the **Find What** box and **01779** into the **Replace With** box.   The current field should be selected to search in and the **Match Whole Field** check box should not be checked.

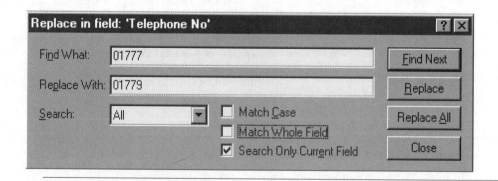

10 Click on the **Replace All** button.

11 Answer ▌Yes▐ to continue.   Note that at this point you could abandon the operation.

12 Now replace all 01779 codes with *01777*.

13 Select the last record, which you have just created, and delete it.

Customising the datasheet layout

Adjusting column widths

To improve the datasheet display, it is possible to alter the widths of the columns. Usually columns are made smaller, as field widths often err on the large side, and this is easily achieved especially if you are familiar with Windows applications.

To alter a column width.

1   Move the pointer to the Field Name row (at the top of the table).

2   Move the pointer to the dividing line between the column you wish to change and the column to the right, it should change shape to a ✛ .

3   Click and drag the column to the desired width.

Adjusting row heights

Another way in which more fields can be displayed across the screen is by increasing the row height. Instead of widening a column to see all the data in a field, if the row height is increased the data in the field will wrap.

To alter a row height.

1   Move the pointer to the row selector (at the left edge of table).

2   Move the pointer to the dividing line between the row you wish to change and the row below, it should change shape to a ✢ .

3   Click and drag the row to the desired height. Note all rows take on the new height.

Changing the font used in the datasheet

Choose Format-Font and select the required font and size from the Font dialog box.

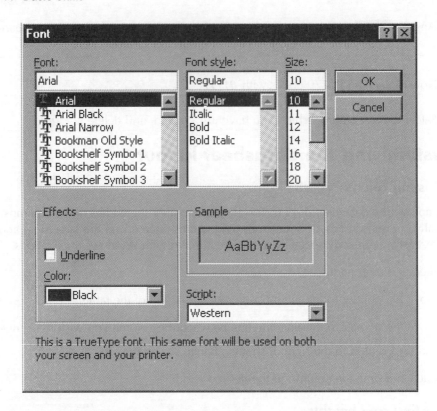

Changing and reorganising fields

You may find it necessary to change a field data type as the design of your database develops or if you import data into it. Before you make any changes to field data types make a backup copy of your database in case you accidentally lose data.

Before you make changes consider the following implications:

■ **Numeric fields**

 Changing from one data type to another that can hold a larger number is generally safe, for example changing a data type of Byte to that of Integer (refer back to Unit 4 for definitions of field size). If on the other hand you change to a data type that holds a smaller number, for example changing from Double to Integer, then your data will be truncated, in this case by losing the decimal part of the number. Truncation means reducing the number of digits in a number to fit the new field size property that you choose.

You cannot convert any type of field into a Counter type field as Access provides automatic numbering in this field type.

■ **Text fields**

 The field size of text fields may be altered but if the alteration is to make the field size smaller text may be truncated. Text fields may be converted to Memo fields but if a Memo field is converted to a text field it will be truncated to 255 characters.

■ **Conversion between data types**

It is possible to convert a field from one data type to another.

■ **Primary key or fields used in relationships**

You cannot change the data type or field size property of these fields.

To change a field data type, make a backup copy of your table, display the design view of your table and make the necessary alterations.

Reorganising fields

If you consider that the order in which the fields are shown in the datasheet needs rearranging, then this can easily be achieved using a drag and drop method. First select the column you wish to move (click on the field name); the pointer then changes shape to a left-pointing arrow. Click and drag the column to a new position. A darker column dividing line will indicate where the field will go when the mouse button is released.

When you close the table you can choose whether or not to make the rearrangement permanent by selecting **Yes** or **No** in the message box.

Displaying data in sorted order

The data displayed in a datasheet will be displayed in the order in which the records were entered. This may not be the order in which you would like to see them and you can control the order of the records using the **Sort Ascending** and **Sort Descending** buttons on the toolbar.

To change the displayed order of the records using one field.

1 Select a column by which you wish to sort (click on the field name at the top of the column).

2 Click on either the **Sort Ascending** or **Sort Descending** button.

To change the displayed order of the records using more than one field.

1 Select the columns by which you wish to sort (click on the field name at the top of the first column and drag to the last column). Sorting columns must be next to one another with the highest priority being assigned to the leftmost column. If necessary rearrange the columns in the datasheet.

2 Click on either the **Sort Ascending** or **Sort Descending** button.

Task 2: Customising the membership datasheet

The aim of this task is to see how columns of data may be re-arranged and also how to adjust their width.

1 Display the **Membership** datasheet.

2   Adjust the widths of the columns to accommodate the data displayed.

3   Select the **Sporting Interests** column and drag it to between the **Occupation** and the **Date of Birth** columns.

4   Close the table without making the rearrangement permanent by choosing No in the message box when closing the table.

Task 3: Displaying records in sorted order

In this task you will view the records in the **Membership** table in different orders.

1   Open the **Membership** table in Datasheet View.

2   Select the **Lastname** column and click on the Sort Ascending button. Click on the Sort Descending button.

3   Try this for other fields in the table.

4   Select the **Category No** and **Lastname** columns together and click on the Sort Ascending button. Note the effect.

5   Drag the **Town** column so it is to the right of the **Category No** column, select these two columns, and click on the Sort Ascending button.

6   Drag the **Town** column so it is to the left of the **Category No** column, select these two columns, and click on the Sort Ascending button. Note the difference between these last two sorts.

7   Close the **Membership** table without saving the layout changes.

Printing a table

You can print a table from its datasheet. Access prints a datasheet as it appears on the screen. For large datasheets, Microsoft Access prints from left-to-right and then from top-to-bottom. For example, if your datasheet is three pages wide and two pages long, Microsoft Access prints the top three pages first, then the bottom three pages. You should preview your datasheet before printing by choosing **File-Print Preview** or clicking on the Preview button in the toolbar.

If you need to set up your printer, choose the Setup button in the **Print** dialog box.

To print a table datasheet

1   Display the table datasheet.

2   If you intend to print selected records, select those records. To print all the records, select nothing.

3   Choose **File-Print Preview,** and if the preview is satisfactory choose **File-Print** to display the **Print** dialog box.

4   Under **Print Range,** choose one of the following:

   • **All,** to print all of the records in the table.

   • **Pages,** to print specific pages from your table.

   • **Selected Record**(s), to print the selected records.

   If you select **Pages,** specify the page numbers of the first and last pages you want to print.

5   Set other **Print** dialog box options if necessary.

6   Choose **OK** .

Task 4: Printing the membership table

1   Display the **Membership** table datasheet.

2   Choose **File-Print Preview,** and then select **File-Print** to display the **Print** dialog box.

3   Under **Print Range** select **All** and click on **OK** .

4   Close the table.

Reviewing data entry and management

What you will learn in this unit

This unit reviews and offers further practice on the following topics:

- entering data
- editing data
- customising the datasheet
- printing a table.

Task 1: Entering and editing data

1 Open the **Chelmer Estates** database and open the **Properties** table in Datasheet View.

2 Enter the data shown in Unit 25 Quick Reference: Data for tables into the **Properties** table.

3 Move between records, and copy, paste and delete fields and records as appropriate.

Task 2: Customising the datasheet

1 Display the **Properties** datasheet

2 Adjust the widths of the columns to accommodate the data displayed.

3 Select the **Date of Entry** and **Selling Price** fields and drag them to insert them after the **Property No** field, so that the three fields are in the order: **Property No**, **Date of Entry**, **Selling Price**.

Property No	Date of Entry	Selling Price	Address	Town	House Type
3	12 June 1995	£100,000.00	3, Bude Close	Chelmer	3
4	20 September 1995	£50,000.00	56, Bodmin Drive	Chelmer	3
5	01 October 1995	£111,000.00	187, Dairyground Road	Chelmer	2
6	21 October 1995	£55,000.00	2, Woodford Road	Meriton	4
7	18 November 1995	£45,000.00	16, The Close	Branford	3
8	04 December 1995	£87,000.00	67, Seal Road	Chelmer	3
9	15 December 1995	£89,000.00	258, Chelmer Lane	Meriton	2
10	02 January 1996	£35,000.00	34, Adelaide Road	Chelmer	5
11	05 January 1996	£150,000.00	345, Chelmer Lane	Chelmer	3
12	05 January 1996	£200,000.00	16, Park Road	Chelmer	1
13	10 January 1996	£300,000.00	4, The Crescent	Branford	2
14	12 January 1996	£115,000.00	66, Dairyground Road	Chelmer	2
15	04 April 1996	£80,000.00	15, Pownall Lane	Chelmer	1
16	03 May 1996	£60,000.00	158, Moss Lane	Chelmer	1
17	21 May 1996	£65,000.00	34, The Grove	Chelmer	4
18	20 June 1996	£45,000.00	Flat 1, Gracelands	Woodford	5
19	21 June 1996	£400,000.00	14, Holly Road	Branford	2
20	29 June 1996	£39,000.00	Flat 4, 346, Chelmer Lane	Chelmer	5
21	04 July 1996	£67,000.00	4, St Paul's Avenue	Chelmer	3
22	15 August 1996	£250,000.00	Oaklands, The Crescent	Branford	2
23	09 September 1996	£120,000.00	18, Merrylands	Branford	2

4   Close the table without making the rearrangement permanent.

Task 3: Printing the Properties table

1   Display the **Properties** table

2   Select the notes column and click on the ▐ **Spelling** ▌ button to check your spellings in the **Notes** field. Operate the spell checker as for a word processor such as Word.

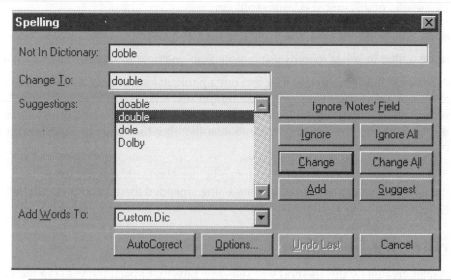

3   Print all of the **Properties** table

4   Close the **Chelmer Estates** database.

Using filters to select records

What you will learn in this unit

Access provides two methods for selecting data, which are known as filtering and querying. Querying is the most useful method and queries are an integral part of the database. Filtering is less useful but is a quick method that allows you to view a selected set of data. You may therefore omit this unit and move directly to the next one, which introduces queries. If you do decide to follow this unit then it would be useful to revisit it after you have completed the units on queries to appreciate the similarities and differences of the two methods.

 Filters are used in conjunction with tables, queries and forms as a means of displaying selected records. A filter will 'filter out' only those records that match specified criteria and only display these records. When a filter is created it is stored with the table, query or form and can quickly allow the user to view data using the filter criteria without having to resort to creating a query. Trends in data may be identified using this method of data filtering. Information concerning, for example, poor membership in a certain category, or property category can easily obtained. Only one filter is stored with the table, query or report but it may be changed if necessary. If you make changes to a filter and do not want to save them, then when you close the table, query or form say No to the save changes question.

By the end of this unit you will be able to:

■ use a filter to select records using one field as a criterion (Filter by Selection)

■ use a filter to select records using more than one field as criteria (Filter by Form).

A common business need is to select out a particular set of data, e.g. a list of customers of a particular type, say, small businesses. A datasheet displays all the records in its underlying table, and by attaching a filter only selected records will be displayed. Using the buttons on the toolbar the filter can easily be switched on or off.

The advantage a filter offers is that it can be designed very quickly whilst viewing the form, table or query. If records are being amended then it can be useful to select certain records, for example, to change a room for a particular activity.

Filter by Selection

A filter created by this method will select records that match the value of the field selected. To filter by this method.

1 Select a field displaying a value that is your criterion, e.g. Meriton in the **Town** field, by clicking in the field to place the insertion point in it. Click on the

button in the toolbar. The filter control buttons are shown below:

 Filter by Selection

Remove/Apply Filter

 2 Only the records with that value in the field will be displayed. To sort the records displayed via the filter use the sorting buttons on the toolbar as described in Unit 7.

3 To remove the filter click on the **Remove Filter** button. Note that once the filter is removed this button becomes an **Apply Filter** button and can be used to re-apply the filter.

Task 1: Selecting with a Filter

In this task you will filter the Membership table to display only those records where the Town field is Meriton.

1 Open the **Chelmer Leisure** database.

2 Open the **Membership** table in Datasheet view.

3 Click in a **Town** field that has the value **Meriton** and click on the **Filter by Selection** button.

4 Only the Meriton records are displayed.

5 Click on the **Remove Filter** button to display all the records. Close the table. You need not save changes, if you do the filter details are saved and can be used next time the table is opened.

Filter by Form

A filter created by this method will select records that match the value of more than one field. Alternatives may be included, for example, Meriton and Bransford in the **Town** field.

 Filter by Form

To filter by this method.

1 Click on the **Filter by Form** button in the toolbar. This displays a filter form. The one illustrated below is for the **Membership** table.

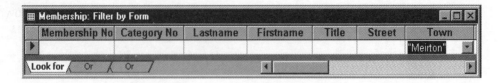

2 Using the filter form specify the criteria for record selection. When you select a field you can open a drop down list, which displays all the different values used for that field in the underlying data.

3 You may specify 'and' criteria by setting values in one or more fields, say all men in category 1.

 4 You may specify 'or' criteria using the 'Or' tab. This will display another sheet of the form filter. The rules of 'and' and 'or' logic for data selection are the same as for queries and are discussed in Unit 11.

5 Click on the **Apply Filter** button on the toolbar.

6 To remove the filter click on the **Remove Filter** button.

Task 2: Selecting with a Filter Form

In this task you will use the **Membership** table and apply a filter to it. Open the **Membership** table in datasheet view. The filter buttons should be in the toolbar. To select records using a filter form.

1 Click on the **Filter by Form** button and the filter form window appears.

2 In the **Town** field select Branford. Click on the **Or** tab and select Meriton.

3 Click on the **Apply Filter** button to display the selected records.

4 To order the records by **Category No** select the category number field and click on the **Sort Ascending** or **Sort Descending** button.

Editing a filter

If you create a filter using Filter by Selection this filter will be saved with the form. To change it to use a different field value for selection purposes simply select that field value and click on the **Filter by Selection** button. If you wish to filter by form instead then click on the **Filter by Form** button and specify your criteria in the form.

The same procedure is used to edit a filter that was created using the filter by form technique.

Task 3: Editing a Filter

This task follows on from Task 2.

1   Click on the **Filter by Form** button to redisplay the form filter.

2   Remove the town criteria by deleting them. Set criteria in the **Category No** field to filter out categories 3 or 4.

3   Click on the **Apply Filter** button to see the records.

4   Experiment with different filter forms, selecting using criteria for different fields.

5   Close the table without saving the changes.

Introducing queries

What you will learn in this unit

This unit introduces the ability of databases to be able to answer questions asked of them. The information stored in a database is of no use unless it can be retrieved in a way so as to be useful. Data stored in a telephone directory can be retrieved, for example, by knowing someone's name and address and using the database (directory) to find out the telephone number.

By the end of this unit you will be able to:

■ question the database by creating a query

■ view the result of the query

■ save a query so that it can be retrieved for later use

■ print out your query.

The role of queries

There are many reasons for using queries; they have a very important role in database systems. Queries are used:

■ so that on-line search and retrieval of specific records can be made. For example, to look at particular set of members for editing, to view the bookings for a given room on a certain day, or to find the class tutors who have a particular qualification

■ for creating forms and printing reports. Queries retrieve a particular set of records and fields; reports are used to print this information. A form based on a query can be used to restrict data entry to certain fields. Units 13 to 23 introduce forms and reports.

All the queries for the **Chelmer Leisure** database will be based on the Membership table. In more sophisticated databases queries may based on more than one table. Unit 24 introduces this concept.

The Simple Query Wizard and Query Design window

Creating a query involves two aspects:

■ selecting the fields to be shown in the query. It is not usually necessary to retrieve all fields, for example a member's name and telephone number may be all that is needed for a telephone survey of a particular group of members

- selecting the records to be shown in the query. For this Access provides a method of querying by which you can describe the characteristics of the data that you are looking for. This method is know as Query By Example (QBE) and is achieved by allowing you to give examples of the data that you are searching for in the form of criteria.

Simple Query Wizard

The Simple Query Wizard helps you design a simple select query. A select query will select fields from a table. The Wizard will ask you to select the table you wish to query and ask which fields you want in your query. It will create the query, which you can then modify later using the Query Design window.

Query Design window

The Query Design window allows a query to be designed that will select the required fields and records that you ask for. This window is in two sections. The upper section displays the field lists of the tables used in the query. In the lower section is a grid for the query design. The two most important rows in the grid are Field and Criteria. Each column needs a field name and you can choose all or some of the fields in the table. In the Criteria row you can give an example of the data. As you work your way through this session you will be introduced to the function of the other rows in the grid.

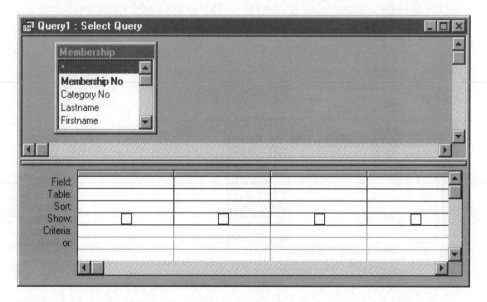

FIGURE 10.1 Query Design window

Before asking questions of a database you must decide which tables in the database are required to answer them. The following activities will describe how to ask questions of just one table: the Membership table. You will see later, in Unit 24, how to include more than one table in a query.

Displaying the Query Design window

1   Click on the **Queries** tab in the Database window and click on the **New** button to create a new query. If you have not created any queries yet then the **Open** and **Design** buttons are not available.

2   Select Design View in the New Query dialog box and click on **OK**.

3   The Show Table dialog box appears in front of the query design window. This dialog box allows you to select all the tables needed for the query. Select a table and click **Add** to add it to the query. When the selection of table(s) is complete click on the **Close** button.

Using the Simple Query Wizard to add fields to a query

After choosing Simple Query Wizard from the New Query dialog box the Simple Query Wizard dialog box is displayed.

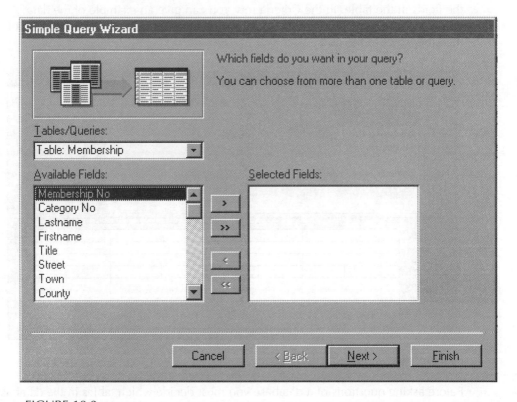

FIGURE 10.2

1   From the Table/Queries drop down list box select the table that the query is to be based on.

2 If you wish to add all the fields to the query click on the ▓ >> ▓ button. If you want to add a selected set of fields highlight each field and click on the ▓ > ▓ button. You may change your mind and use the ▓ << ▓ button to remove all fields (so you may start again) or use the ▓ < ▓ button to remove a selected field.

3 When the required fields have been chosen click on ▓Next>▓. Select a Detail query and click on ▓Next>▓. Give the query a title and click on ▓Finish▓. The result of your query will be shown in Datasheet view.

Task 1: Selecting fields for a query using Simple Query Wizard

1 From the **Chelmer Leisure** database window click on the ▓Queries▓ tab and click on the ▓New▓ button. Choose the Simple Query Wizard from the New Query dialog box.

2 From the Table/Queries drop down list box in the Simple Query Wizard dialog box select the **Membership** table.

3 Add the fields **Membership No**, **Lastname**, **Sex**, and **Date of Joining** to the query by highlighting each field in turn and clicking on the ▓ > ▓ button.

4 Click on ▓Next>▓. Select a Detail query and click on ▓Next>▓. Give the query the title *Dates of Joining* and click on ▓Finish▓. The result of your query will be shown in Datasheet view. View and close the query window, the name of the query is listed in the Database window.

Adding fields to a query without using the Wizard

By choosing Design View from the New Query dialog box the Show Table box will be displayed in front of the query design window. After choosing the table for the query the table's field list box will be displayed in the upper section of the query design window as seen in Figure 10.1. The next step is to decide which fields in that table you wish to include in the query. Later we will explore query criteria that allow us to select specific records. The query is designed in the lower section of the query design window.

Adding all the fields in the table to the query

The simplest case is where we want to include all the fields in the table.

1 Double click on the title bar of the field list box of the table in the upper section of the window. This selects all the fields.

2 Click on any of the selected fields (not the *) and drag to the field cell in the lower section of the Query window. The pointer should look like a set of record cards.

3 When you release the mouse button all the field names will have been added to the query. Use the horizontal scroll bar to move to the right, as not all the columns will fit on the screen.

Adding individual fields in the table to the query

There are three other ways of adding the fields one by one to a query.

The first method is by double-clicking.

1 Double-click on the name of the field required in the field list box in the upper section of the window. It will appear in the next available column in the grid below.

The second is to use the drop down list associated with each field cell.

1 Click in the field cell in the lower section of the window. A list box button appears at the end of the cell.

2 Click on the list box button and a drop down list of field names will appear.

3 Select the name of the field required, if necessary scroll through the list, click on it and it will appear in the field cell.

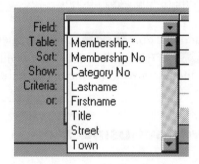

The third way is to use the drag-and-drop method.

1 Click on the name of the field required in the field list box in the upper section of the window.

2 Drag and drop this field into the required field cell in the lower part of the Query window. While doing this, the pointer should look like one record card.

3 If you drop the field onto a column containing a field, then a column will be inserted to contain the new field.

Removing fields from the query

Fields may be removed singly or in blocks from the query. To remove all the fields from the query.

1 Select the first column by clicking on the bar at the top of the column, (the pointer will change shape to a down arrow) drag to select all the columns.

2   Press the *Delete* key or choose **Edit-Delete**.

To remove an individual field from the query, just select the required column for deleting and use **Edit-Delete**.

Viewing or running a query

To see the result of a query, either click on the **Datasheet** button or the **Run Query** button in the toolbar. To return to the query design click on the **Design** button next to the **Datasheet** button in the toolbar.

Design button   Datasheet button   Run Query button

Access displays a datasheet containing the records that match the query with fields as defined in the query. Access calls this query result a dynaset. A dynaset is a temporary table and is not a permanent part of your database. If you modify your query the resulting dynaset will change accordingly.

Task 2: Selecting fields for a query

In this task you will query the **Membership** table and data from all records will be shown in the dynasets. Initially all fields will be shown and then you will see how to select only certain fields.

1   Starting from the Database window, click on the **Queries** tab.

2   Click on **New** to open a new query, and choose **Design View**.

3   Select the table **Membership** from the **Show Table** dialog box and close the dialog box.

4   Add all the fields to the query (as described in the previous section).

5   Click on the **Datasheet** button in the toolbar. You should see the whole of the table forming the dynaset.

6   Click on the **Design** button in the toolbar to return to the Query Design window.

7   Remove all the fields from the query (as described in the previous section).

8   Add the fields **Membership No**, **Lastname**, **Sex**, **Date of Joining** individually to the query, experimenting with the different methods described.

9   Click on the **View** or **Run Query** button in the toolbar, you should see only these fields from all the records of the table forming the dynaset.

10 Click on the **View** button in the toolbar to return to the Query Design window.

11 By adding and removing fields alter the fields in your query so that they are **Lastname**, **Sex**, **Category No**, **Sporting Interests**.

12 Click on the **View** button in the toolbar, or the **Run Query** button and you should see only these fields from all the records of the table forming the dynaset.

13 Move on to the next task or close the query without saving.

Task 3: More practice in selecting fields for a query

1 Create a series of queries showing all of the records in the database, but including only the following fields:

■ **Membership No**, **Surname**, **Forenames**, **Telephone No**

■ **Membership No**, **Date of Joining**

■ **Occupation**

2 Examine each of the dynasets in turn. Do not save these queries. Discuss circumstances in which each of these lists may be useful.

Saving a query

Sometimes you may wish to ask the same question of a database over and over again, for example, is a membership subscription due? As time passes members need to renew their membership and it is useful to be able to send reminders. A query designed to do this would be saved so that it can be used repeatedly. To save a query.

1 Choose **File-Save**.

2 In the **Query Name** box of the **Save As** dialog box enter a name that will remind you what the query is about. The name can be up to 255 characters. Click on **OK**.

3 If you close the Query window, you will see the name of your query in the queries list of the Database window, from where it can be opened for use on another occasion.

Closing and opening a query

To close a query, either double-click on the query's control menu button, or choose **File-Close**.

You can open an existing query in either Design View or Datasheet View.

To open a query in Design View:

1 In the Database window, click on the **Queries** tab.

2 Select the query you want to open, and then click on the **Design** button.

To open a query in Datasheet View:

1 In the Database window, click on the **Query** button.

2 Select the query you want to open, and then click on the **Open** button.

Task 4: Saving a query

1 Recreate the query described at the end of Task 2.

2 Choose **File-Save** or click on the **Save** button.

3 Give the name ***Members' Sporting Interests*** to this query and click on **OK** .

4 Close the query and you should see the name of the query in the Database window.

Printing a query

Before printing the dynaset produced by your query it is advisable to preview it. To preview a query table:

1 In the Datasheet View, click on the **Print Preview** button on the toolbar. You will be shown a preview, which displays a miniature version of what is to be printed.

2 The pointer becomes a magnifying glass and can be use to zoom-in to the page. If you use other Windows applications you will be familiar with this. Clicking will 'toggle' between zoom-in and zoom-out modes. When zoomed-in the vertical and horizontal scroll bars can be used to scroll around your previewed page.

3 To adjust the column widths you need to return to the datasheet view. To do this click on the **Close** button. The column widths are adjusted in the same way as for table datasheets as described in Unit 7.

Once you are satisfied that the preview is correct, then from the Print Preview mode:

1 Choose **File-Print**. The **Print** dialog box appears. If you want to print without changing anything then skip the following three steps. To print directly, without displaying the **Print** dialog box, click on the **Print** button in the toolbar.

2 In the **Print** dialog box click on the **Setup** button and the **Page Setup** dialog box appears.

3 To change the margins click in the appropriate box and edit the default setting. You can select the orientation of the page, the printer and the paper size. The **Print Headings** check box, if not checked, will suppress the printing of the field names as headings. Click on **OK** to return to the **Print** dialog box.

4 Click on **OK** . Click on the **Close** button to return to the query datasheet.

Task 5: Printing

In this task you will print the dynaset produced by the query saved in Task 4.

1 From the Database window open the Members' Sporting Interests query in Datasheet view.

2 Click on the **Print Preview** button on the toolbar.

3 Some columns may need widening. Click on **Close** to return to the datasheet and widen the columns (see Unit 7).

4 Preview again, zoom in to check that the columns are wide enough, click on the **Print** button.

5 Click on **OK** in the **Print** dialog box and the dynaset, FIGURE 10.3, should be printed.

6 Click on the **Close** button to return to the datasheet view.

Lastname	Sex	Category No	Sporting Interests
Walker	Male	2	Tennis, squash
Cartwright	Female	1	Aerobics, swimming, running, squash
Perry	Male	6	Judo, Karate
Forsythe	Female	2	
Jameson	Female	1	Aerobics, squash
Robinson	Female	3	Swimming, Judo
Harris	Male	5	Badminton, cricket
Shangali	Male	2	Weight training
Barrett	Female	1	Keep fit, swimming
Weiner	Male	1	Weight training, squash
Ali	Male	6	Judo, swimming, football
Young	Female	2	Keep fit, Aerobics, squash
Gray	Male	5	
Swift	Female	5	
Davies	Female	1	Aerobics, squash, swimming
Robinson	Female	1	Tennis, Aerobics
Everett	Male	2	Squash, Fitness training, football
Locker	Male	4	
Locker	Female	4	
Jones	Male	1	Weight training

FIGURE 10.3

Deleting a query

Queries that will be used more than once should be saved but a query may have a limited usefulness or be superseded. Therefore, from time to time some queries will need to be removed.

However, care needs to be taken when removing a query. Later, we will see that reports and forms can be based upon queries, so it is important to assign these to alternative queries or to delete them as well. At present there is nothing based on the queries we have created and they may be deleted safely.

To delete a query, in the Database window click on the **Queries** tab to display the queries. Highlight the query that is to be deleted and press the *Delete* key.

Task 6: Deleting a query

In this task the query created using the Simple Query Wizard will be deleted.

1 Display the queries in the Database window.

2 Select the query created by the Wizard, **Dates of Joining** and press the *Delete* key.

3 Reply **Yes** to confirm the delete operation.

Using query criteria

What you will learn in this unit

There are many reasons for asking questions. In business, questions are important in decision making. Questioning data relating to, for example, marketing or management, can be very effective using a database management system. In the case of Chelmer Leisure and Recreation Centre questions can help with decisions such as:

■ does the centre attract mainly local members; what is the effect of local competition?

■ no-smoking areas being introduced

■ introducing activities and facilities for older members

■ introducing a discount scheme for loyal members

■ fees charged for various categories.

To ask questions you need to test criteria. These criteria are entered into the criteria cells of the Query design grid. Querying is done by example, so an example of the answer to the question is entered into the criteria cell.

By the end of this unit you will be able to:

■ enter query criteria

■ rename and hide fields in a query

■ use logic in queries.

Entering query criteria

Query criteria basically allow the enquirer to frame questions, which enable specific records to be retrieved from the database. We might want to find out various things using the data stored in a table. For example, some questions that might be asked about the **Membership** table are:

■ which members live in Chelmer?

■ which members smoke?

■ which members are over 60?

■ which members joined before 1/1/92?

■ which members are in categories 1 and 2?

Task 1: Query criteria for the membership table

In this task the above questions will be formulated as queries for the **Membership** table. The queries use the datatypes Text, Number, Date and Yes/No. Each question will be dealt with in turn.

1   Create a new query using the **Membership** table.

2   Add all the fields to the query.

Which members live in Chelmer?

3   In the Criteria cell of the **Town** field type *Chelmer*.

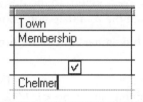

4   Click on the **Datasheet** or **Run Query** button.

The resulting dynaset should only contain records for which the **Town** field is equal to Chelmer.

5   Return to the design view. Notice that Access puts double quotes around your criterion if it thinks it is text. Delete the criterion "Chelmer". Select the cell by double-clicking and press *Delete* to clear the cell. Alternatively click in the cell and use the *Backspace* key to delete the criterion.

Which members smoke?

6   In the Criteria cell of the **Smoker** field type *Yes*

You may need to scroll to the right to display this cell on the screen.

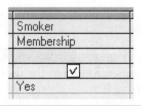

7   Click on the **Datasheet** or **Run Query** button and view the resulting dynaset.

8   Return to the design view. Delete the last criterion.

Which members are over 60?

9   In the Criteria cell of the **Date of**
    Birth field type *<1/1/37*.

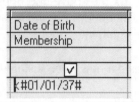

10 Click on the **Datasheet** or **Run Query** button and view the resulting
   dynaset. Return to the design view. Notice that Access has recognised your query
   example as a date and converted it to <#01/01/37#. Delete this criterion.

Which members joined before 1/1/92?

11 In the Criteria cell of the **Date of**
   Joining field type *<1/1/92*.

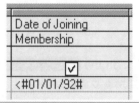

12 Click on the **Datasheet** or **Run Query** button and view the resulting
   dynaset. Return to the design view. Delete this criterion.

Which members are in categories 1 and 2?

13 In the Criteria cell of the **Category No**
   field type *<=2*.

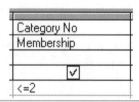

14 Click on the **Datasheet** or **Run Query** button and view the resulting
   dynaset. Return to the design view. Delete this criterion. Close the query without
   saving it.

Renaming and hiding fields in a query

When queries are printed it is sometimes necessary to widen the column so that the
field name at the top of the column can be seen. This in turn can lead to unneces-
sarily wide columns, so it is useful to be able to rename the field. The field header
can be renamed in a query, for example, **Last Renewed** instead of **Date of Last**
Renewal.

Note: renaming the field header does not affect the name of the field in the underlying table.

To change field header names.

1 Switch to query design mode by clicking on the Query Design button. Move the insertion point to the column containing the field header name you wish to change.

2 Point to the beginning of the field header and click. The aim is to put the flashing insertion point at the beginning of the header name.

If you accidentally select the header, press *F2* to de-select it. If the insertion point is not at the beginning, then press the *Home* key to move it to the first character position.

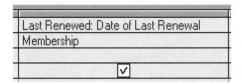

3 Type in the new name for the field, and follow the name with a colon. Do not put a space between the name and the colon. The colon separates the name you type from the existing field name, which moves to the right to make room for your addition.

4 Click on the Datasheet button or the Run Query button and the query result with amended field header will be displayed.

In this and the previous unit you have seen how to select the fields you want to see in the result of a query and how to impose criteria. These can be combined so that the dynaset contains only the records that match the criteria and only the fields specified in the query. To be able to impose a criterion on a field, that field needs to be in the Query grid, which means that it will form part of the dynaset. This may not always be desirable so Access offers the choice of whether or not the field forms part of the dynaset. By default all fields in the query appear in the dynaset as the Show cell is active. To hide a field click in the box in the Show cell. The tick disappears and the field will not form part of the dynaset.

Task 2: Renaming and hiding fields in a query

Query 1

The following query lists the names and addresses of all the male members who are smokers.

1 Create a new query using the **Membership** table.

2 Add the following fields: **Membership No**, **Title**, **Lastname**, **Street**, **Town**, **County**, **Post Code**, **Smoker**, **Sex**.

3 In the criteria fields of **Smoker** and **Sex** put ***Yes***. Hide these fields.

4 Sort the **Lastname** field in ascending order.

5 Rename **Membership No** as ***Member No*** and display the dynaset.

Member No	*Title*	*Lastname*	*Street*	*Town*	*County*	*Post Code*
13	Mr	Gray	4 The Parade	Chelmer	Cheshire	CH1 7ER
7	Mr	Harris	55 Coven Road	Chelmer	Cheshire	CH3 8PS
20	Mr	Jones	17 Mayfield Avenue	Chelmer	Cheshire	CH2 9OL
1	Mr	Walker	16 Dovecot Close	Chelmer	Cheshire	CH2 6TR

6 Save the query as ***Addresses of Male Smokers***. Close the query.

Query 2

In this task you will create a query which looks at the occupations of the female members of the centre. The result of this query will be selected fields from selected records.

1 Create a new query using the **Membership** table.

2 Add the following fields to the query: **Category No**, **Firstname**, **Lastname**, **Occupation**, **Sex**.

3 In the criteria cell of the **Sex** field type ***No***.

4 Click on the check box in the Show cell of the **Sex** field to hide it.

5 Click at the beginning of the **Category No** Header and type ***Cat:*** (do not type a space before the colon).

6 Click on the **Datasheet** or **Run Query** button to view the result of the query. The **Category No** field should have the header **Cat** and the **Sex** field should be hidden.

7 Save the query as ***Occupations of Female Members***.

Exploring types of query criteria

The queries that have been created so far in this unit have only used criteria in one field. Criteria may be applied to all the fields included in a query. Each field may be sorted or hidden. By combining these options more complex queries can be produced.

We have already used some of the operators used in criteria. Table 11.1 summarises them.

Operator	Meaning
Mathematical operators	
<	less than
>	greater than
<>	not equal to
>=	greater than or equal to
<=	less than or equal to
+	addition
-	subtraction
*	multiplication
/	division
Text operators	
"J*"	text strings beginning with J
"*ton"	text strings ending with ton
"*k*"	text strings containing the letter k

TABLE 11.1 Operators used in criteria

You may have noticed that after running a query, if you return to the query design, that Access modifies the criteria slightly, for example enclosing dates in hashes. Text criteria may be entered using no quotes, single quotes or double quotes. Access will convert a text criterion entered without quotes so that it is enclosed in double quotes. If you use one of the text operators in TABLE 11.1, then typing "*k*", '*k*', or *k* would produce the same result and Access would convert *k* to "*k*".

Using logic in queries

In a query you can use criteria in more than one field, for example male smokers (Query 1 in Task 2). The question is "Is the member male AND does he smoke?" There is a logical AND between the two criteria; both criteria must be true for the record to be retrieved.

What if a logical AND is required on the same field, for example members whose date of joining was after 1/1/92 AND before the 1/1/93 (Query 2 in Task 3 below)? In the criteria cell the word "and" is used between the two criteria, for example **>=1/1/92 and <1/1/93**. You can specify more than two criteria but remember to put the word AND between them.

The other form of logic used in queries is OR. There is a row entitled or: in the query design grid for OR criteria to be entered. An example would be a query which requires as its answer the names and addresses of members who live in Chelmer OR Meriton. To set up this query enter **Chelmer** into the criteria row of the

Town field and *Meriton* in the or: row. The example query below (Task 3, Query 3) lists the names of the members who are likely to use the fitness suite, as their sporting interests are aerobics, fitness training or weight training.

Task 3: Using different types of query criteria

Query 1 - Querying text fields

This query picks out people with particular sporting interests

1   Create a new query using the **Membership** table.

2   Add the following fields: **Membership No**, **Lastname**, **Category No**, **Sporting Interests**.

3   In the criteria fields of Sporting Interests type *"*Tennis*"*. Note that Access will convert this to read **Like "*Tennis*"**.

4   Sort the **Lastname** field in ascending order.

5   Rename **Membership No** as *Member No.* and **Category No** as *Cat*.

6   Display and print the dynaset. Save the query giving it the name *Sporting Interest* and close the query.

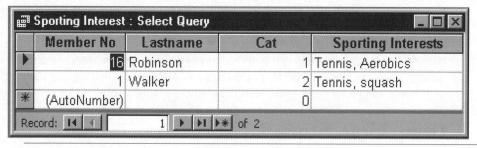

Query 2 - Logic using AND

This query picks out members who joined in 1992.

1   Create a new query using the **Membership** table.

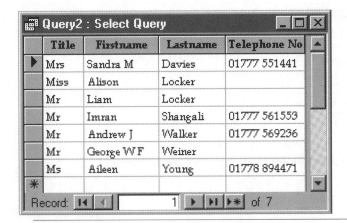

2 Add the following fields: **Title**, **Firstname**, **Lastname**, **Telephone No**, **Date of Joining**.

3 In the criteria field of **Date of Joining** type *>=1/1/92 and <=1/1/93*. Note that Access will convert this to read *>=#01/01/92# And <#01/01/93#*.

4 Hide the **Date of Joining** field.

5 Sort the **Lastname** field in ascending order.

6 Display and print the dynaset. Save the query giving it the name *When joined* and close the query.

Query 3 - Logic using OR

This query picks out members whose sporting interests are aerobics, fitness training or weight training and shows their home town so that local interest can be assessed.

1 Create a new query using the **Membership** table.

2 Add the following fields: **Membership No**, **Category No**, **Lastname**, **Town**, **Sporting Interests**.

3 In the criteria field of **Sporting Interests** type *"*aerobics*"*. Note that Access will convert this to *Like "*aerobics*"*.

4 In the or: field of **Sporting Interests** type *"*fitness training*"*.

5 In the row below type *"*weight training*"*.

6 Hide the **Sporting Interests** field.

7 Sort the **Lastname** field in ascending order.

8 Display the dynaset. Notice that when querying text Access is not case sensitive, "*aerobics*" will find aerobics, AEROBICS or Aerobics. Print the dynaset. Close the query without saving.

Query 3 Unit 11 : Select Query

Member No	Cat	Lastname	Town
2	1	Cartwright	Chelmer
15	1	Davies	Meriton
17	2	Everett	Chelmer
5	1	Jameson	Chelmer
20	1	Jones	Chelmer
16	1	Robinson	Chelmer
8	2	Shangali	Chelmer
10	1	Weiner	Chelmer
12	2	Young	Branford
(AutoNumber)	0		Chelmer

Record: |◄ ◄ | 1 | ► ►| ►* | of 9

Task 4: More practice with query criteria

The following queries can be performed using basic query operators, and do not require the use of logical operators. Create queries to answer each of the following questions. Examine the dynaset created. Hide any fields that should not be shown, either because they are irrelevant or because all records in the dynaset hold the same value. Save each of the queries in turn, under a name of your choice.

1 Which members do not live in Chelmer? Show the following fields for records in the dynaset: **Title**, **Firstname**, **Lastname**, **Street**, **Town**.

2 Which members are female? Display the following fields: **Lastname, Firstname, Telephone No**.

3 Which members joined after 1/6/93? Display **Title, Lastname, Firstname**, and **Date of Joining**.

4 Which members have expressed an interest in aerobics?

The following queries require the use of the logical query operators, AND and OR. Create queries that show all the fields in the record in answer to the following questions.

1 Which members have sporting interests that include either cricket or running? This provides a perspective on those members who are interested in outdoor sports.

2 Which members joined in 1993?

3 Which members are either unemployed, retired, or a housewife? This query identifies members who might be interested in activities during the working day.

4 Which members are interested in both aerobics and squash?

5 Which members are in Junior or Youth categories (3, 4 or 6), and what are their dates of birth?

Reviewing sorting and queries

What you will learn in this unit

This unit reviews and offers further practice on queries, using the Chelmer Estates database. The following topics are covered:

- sorting records
- defining the fields to appear in the output from a query
- creating queries using basic query criteria
- creating queries using logical operators.

Task 1: Sorting the records in a table

This task asks you to experiment with alternative orders for the display of the records.

1 Open the Properties table of the **Chelmer Estates** database in Datasheet View. Sort the records in ascending order of **Selling Price**.

2 Re-sort the records in ascending order according to house type, thereby grouping all properties of a certain type together.

3 If you drag the **Selling Price** column next to the **House Type** column so that the **Selling Price** column is to the right of the **House Type** column, select both columns and click on the **Sort Ascending** button then you should see the records in price order within house type.

Task 2: Filtering records

You may omit this task if you omitted the unit on filtering.

1 Open the **Properties** table in Datasheet View.

2 Click on one of the **Town** fields displaying the town Branford. Click on the **Filter by Selection** button to display all the properties in Branford. Click on the **Remove Filter** button.

3 Click on the **Filter by Form** button. Click on the **Down arrow** button of the **Number of Bedrooms** field and select 2. Repeat this for the **Town** field and select Chelmer. Click on the **Apply Filter** button to view the result.

4 Click on the **Filter by Form** button and edit the filter to look for two-bedroomed houses in Meriton as well as Chelmer. Click on the **Or** tab and set the criteria Meriton for Town and 2 for Number of Bedrooms. Click on the **Apply Filter** button to view the result. Click on the **Remove Filter** button. Close the datasheet. You need not save the changes.

Note that when using OR and multiple criteria you need to take care with logic. In this task we are looking for two-bedroomed houses in Chelmer OR two-bedroomed houses in Meriton. If you omit the number of bedrooms criteria in the OR part of the form, all houses in Meriton, irrespective of the number of bedrooms, will be selected. Try it.

Task 3: Defining the fields to appear in a query output

1 Create a series of queries showing all the records in the database, but including only the following fields:

- **Property No, Address, Town**

- **Property No, Town, House Type and Selling Price**

- **Property No, Address, Notes**.

2 Examine each of the dynasets in turn. Try using sorting in these queries and investigate the difference the field order makes (Unit 7).

3 Do not save these queries. Discuss the circumstances in which each of these lists might be useful.

Task 4: Using basic query criteria

Create a series of queries to answer each of the questions below. Display the following fields for records in the dynaset: **Address**, **House Type**, **Selling Price**. Examine the query dynasets. Save each of the queries in turn, using a name of your choice:

1 Which properties are in Chelmer?

2 Which properties are Detached houses and also Freehold?

3 Which properties have four or more bedrooms?

4 Which properties have a garden that is less than 100 metres in length?

5 Which properties have been on the books (in the system) since before December 1995?

6 Which properties are Detached, have four or more bedrooms, and have a double garage?

7   Which properties have a granny flat?

8   Which properties have gas central heating?

Why would it be useful to be able to conduct such a wide range of different types of queries on the Chelmer Estates database?

Task 5: Queries using logical query operators

The following queries require the use of the logical operators, AND and OR. Create queries that show all of the fields in the record in answer to the following questions:

1   Which properties have a selling price between 80,000 and 100,000?

2   Which properties have either a granny flat or a cloakroom (or both)?

3   Which properties have both a granny flat and a cloakroom?

4   Which properties have either a double garage or five or more bedrooms (or both)?

5   Which properties are either bungalows with four or more bedrooms or have a granny flat?

Screen forms

What you will learn in this unit

In this unit you will learn how to create a screen form. A screen form provides a more user-friendly way to work with your data. Entering data can be made easier and less prone to error.

By the end of the session you will be able to:

■ create a form using Form Wizards

■ save a form

■ use a form

■ print a form.

In Units 2 to 6 you defined the tables for the Chelmer Leisure and Recreation Centre. You entered data into the **Membership** table but have not yet entered data into the **Classes** table. You will do so in this unit. You could enter the data as you did for the **Membership** table, using the Datasheet View of the table. The disadvantage of using the Datasheet View is that the fields in a record often do not all fit on the screen. Also viewing and entering data in the datasheet grid can be somewhat tiresome.

When data is collected manually it is often by means of filling out a form. In a form there are boxes to fill in, for example with name, address, and there may be boxes that are ticked, for example Yes/No boxes. Access offers the facility to create a form on the screen so that data can be entered into a table by filling in the form. Filling in such a form should be more user friendly than filling in the cells in a datasheet provided that the form has been designed carefully. It is usual to have a form for each table of data for the purpose of entering and editing data in that table.

Most fields on a form appear as text boxes, but there may also be check boxes for Yes/No fields, depending on the display control setting (Unit 1). If a Yes/No field has a text box setting, it will display the formats specified, such as Male or Female, and data is entered by typing Yes or No. If the display control is set as a check box data is entered by clicking on the control for Yes and leaving blank for No.

Forms can be used to enter, edit, display and print data contained in your tables. They offer the advantage of presenting data, on screen, in an organised and attractive manner.

Standard forms are created for most applications or jobs, for example a form for entering the details of a new member, as shown in FIGURE 13.1.

Access allows you to create forms to your own design, for which it provides a wide range of tools. If you are a new Access user, or simply for convenience, AutoForm and the Form Wizard provide a quick and easy way to create a basic form. This basic form can be customised later. To enable us to get started quickly on form design we will make use of AutoForm and the Form Wizard.

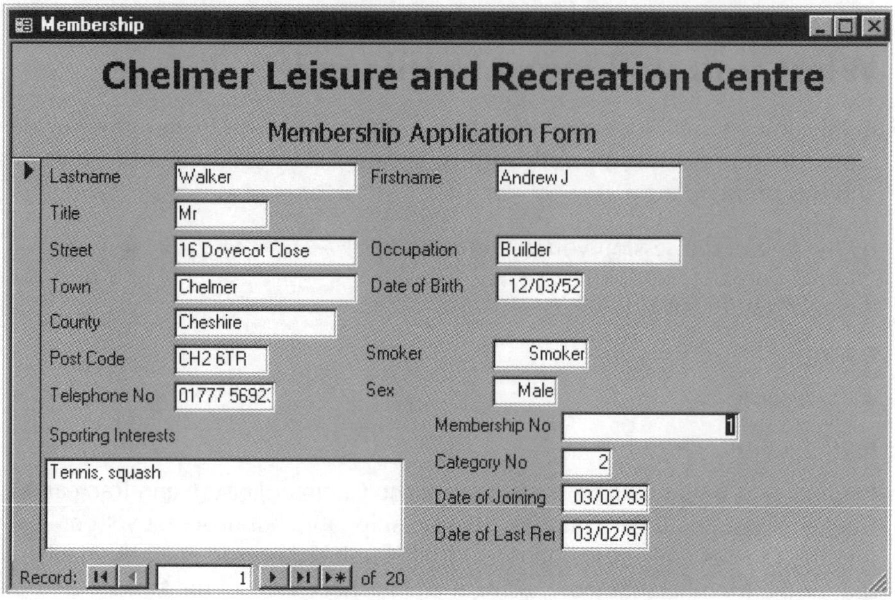

FIGURE 13.1 A form for entering membership data

Creating a form with AutoForm

There are three types of form that can be created using AutoForm:

- Columnar

- Tabular

- Datasheet.

A Columnar form will display data from one record at a time. Tabular and Datasheet forms are very similar in that they display more than one record at once. Due to the tabular format, if there are a lot of fields in the records then an entire record will not fit on the screen.

AutoForm will create a form instantly, using all fields in the records of the underlying table that you choose to base your form upon. To create a form using AutoForm:

1   Starting from the Database window, either:

- click on the **Forms** tab and then click on the **New** button, or

- click on the **New Object** button in the toolbar, select **Form** and a **New Form** dialog box appears.

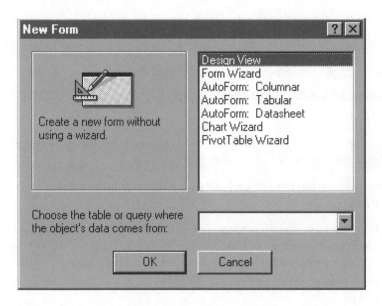

FIGURE 13.2

1 Click on the **list box** button of the **Choose the table or query where the object's data comes from** box, to produce a list of tables and queries and select the table for which you wish to create a form.

2 Select one of the **AutoForm** options and click on **OK**.

Creating a form using Form Wizard

Form Wizard, as well as allowing you to create a columnar, tabular and datasheet form, allows you to create a justified form. A justified form displays one record at a time in a row format. To create a Form Wizard form:

1 Perform steps 1 and 2 above, then select **Form Wizard**, and click on **OK**. Check that the correct table is listed in the **Tables/Queries** box (if it isn't, select the right one).

2 The next stage is to choose which fields are to be on the form. The fields that you can have in the form are shown in the **Available Fields** box.

■ These can be transferred to the **Selected Fields** box by selecting each field in turn and clicking on the **>** button.

■ If you wish to add all the fields in the table to the form then click on the **>>** button.

■ You may set the order in which the fields appear on the form by selecting them in the order you desire. The ⎡ < ⎤ button will remove a highlighted field from a form and ⎡ << ⎤ will remove all the fields from the form.

Once you have added the required fields to the form continue by clicking on the Next> button.

3 Choose whether a Columnar, Tabular, Datasheet or Justified form is required. The layout of these was discussed in the AutoForm activity.

4 You are then asked what kind of look you want for your form and are given a choice of styles.

An example of the look is shown to the left of the dialog box. Click on each style in turn to see what it would look like. The first time you create a form choose Standard, you can modify the style later. You are asked then asked for a title. Key in an appropriate title. Now click on the Finish button to display the form with data in it.

Saving and closing a form

Save a form by choosing **File-Save** or clicking on the Save button. If this is a new form that you have not yet saved then Access will prompt you for a file name with a Save As dialog box. If you wish later to save this form with a different name then use **File-Save As** and fill in the appropriate details in the dialog box.

Remember that there is a distinction between the name and the title of a form. The title is displayed at the top of the form window. The name you give when saving the form is the form's object name, which you need to be able to recognise when you want to open the form for use again. These names appear in the Database window when the Form tab is selected.

A form can be closed by using **File-Close** or by using the Close button of the form window. If the form or the latest modification has not been saved you will be prompted to save. When a form is closed its name (the one you gave to it when saving) will be shown in the database window when you click on the Form tab.

To open a form from the Database window, click on the Form tab, select the name of the form required and click on the Open button.

Task 1: Creating a columnar membership form using AutoForm

In this task you will create a single column membership which can later be modified to look like the form shown in FIGURE 13.1. The order in which you select the fields for the form is important, as will become apparent when the form is used to enter data.

To create this form:

1 From the Chelmer Leisure Database window click on the **Form** tab and click on the **New** button.

2 Open the list box (where data comes from) in the New Form dialog box and select Membership from the list of tables. Select AutoForm: Columnar and click on **OK** .

Access creates a form with a list of field names and corresponding data, which for the fields in the Membership table use two columns. Notice that there are some differences between this form and the one shown in FIGURE 13.1. Customising the form will be considered in Unit 14.

3 Choose File-Save and give the form the name *Membership*.

4 Close the form.

Task 2: Creating a columnar classes form using AutoForm

In this task use AutoForm to create a columnar form for the **Classes** table, as seen in FIGURE 13.3, and save the form as *Classes*.

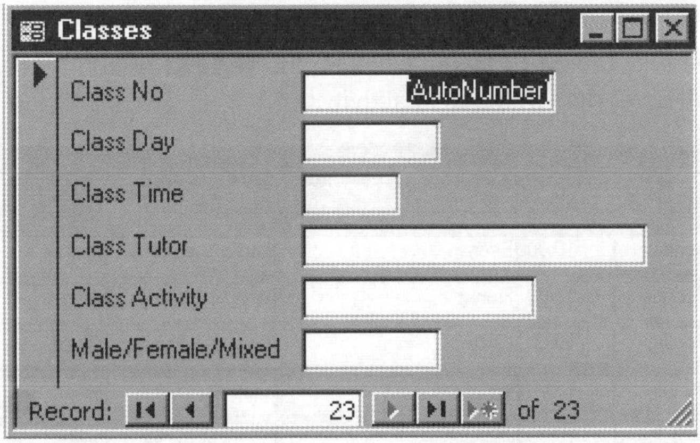

FIGURE 13.3

Creating a tabular form

A tabular form is one that displays more than one record on the screen. The field names form headers for columns and the records are shown below in a table. The number of records displayed will depend upon the size of the window and the number of records in the table. If there are a lot of fields in a record it is unlikely that you will be able to see the complete record on the screen and you will need to scroll to the right to display more of the fields. This type of form is suited to records with only a few fields, such as those in the **Classes** table. The advantage of this form is that it displays more than one record at a time.

A tabular form may be created either using AutoForm or Form Wizard. The following task considers creating a tabular form using the Form Wizard.

Task 3: Creating the classes tabular form

This task will create a tabular classes form.

1   First close any open form.

2   From the Database window with the **Form** tab selected click on **New**.

3   In the New Form dialog box select the **Classes** table.

4   Select **FormWizard** and click on **OK**.

5   Add all the fields to the form and click on the **Next>** button.

6   Choose a **Tabular** form and click on the **Next>** button.

7   Choose a standard style and click on **Next>**.

8   Give the form the title **Table of Classes**. Click on the **Finish** button to display the form. You will enter data in the next activity.

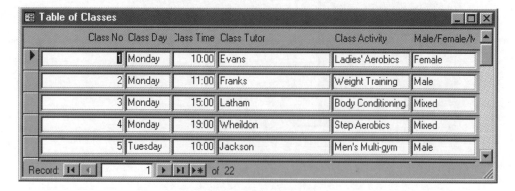

The difference between this form and the single column form is that the fields are arranged in columns. The top of the column is headed by the field name. As you haven't yet entered data into this form, you will see only one blank record. When records have been added, as we shall see later, then more than one record is as illustrated above.

9   Save the form **Table of Classes**.

10 Close the form.

Using a form

To use a form, first display the available forms in the Database window by clicking on the **Form** tab. Open the form either by selecting it and clicking on **Open** or by double clicking on its name.

You can use the form to look at the data in the table (or query) upon which it is based. Whether it is a single column or tabular form use the record movement keys in the status bar or use the **Edit-Go To** menu to move around the records in your form. Using the *Page Up* and *Page Down* keys with a single column form will display the next/previous record whereas with a tabular form they will page up or down a screenful of records.

Using the form to enter a new record into the table

You should design forms with the purpose of entering data into records in mind, as this is their primary function. Entering data is a labour intensive task and the design of the form is important.

To enter a new record using a form.

1   Go to the end of your records using the new record button on the status bar or the tool bar. If your form is single column press the *Page Down* key and a blank form appears. If your form is tabular click in the first field of the blank record shown at the end of your records.

2   Enter data for another record by filling in the boxes for each field. In Access these boxes are called controls. When you have completed each text box (control) press *Enter* or *Tab* to move to the next one.

3   Enter **Yes** or **No** for **Yes/No** fields that have text box display controls and the appropriate word, e.g. Male or Female, will appear.

Task 4: Using a form to enter data into a table

In this task we shall enter data into the categories of **Classes** table, using the tabular form just created.

1   Open either the columnar or tabular form based on **Classes**.

2   Enter the data as given in Unit 25.   You may wish to enter some of the records using one form and the rest using the other type of form. If so, close the form and open the other one. As you enter each record it is saved to the **Classes** table.

3   Close the form when you have finished entering the data.

Printing a form

Forms are designed primarily for screen use, i.e. they are intended for data to be entered via the computer and they display the data on screen. However, Access offers the facility to print from a form. Before printing a form always preview it first. A form can be previewed from either the run or design view mode.

Previewing

 Previewing will display a miniature version of what is to be printed. This allows the layout to be assessed so that adjustments can be made before printing.

To preview a form

1   Click on the **Print Preview** button in the toolbar.

2   To zoom-in and zoom-out simply click anywhere on the preview, or use the **Zoom** button. Clicking on the right mouse button will allow you to select the degree of magnification.

3   Choose **File-Page Setup** to make adjustments such as the orientation (i.e. portrait or landscape), the choice of printer and the width of the margins. Click on **OK** when the required adjustments have been made.

Printing

When satisfied that the preview is correct, printing may be done from either the preview screen or the form screen. To print from the preview screen.

1   Choose **File-Print**.

2   Select whether all or certain pages of the form will be printed and the number of copies. Click on **OK**.

To print from the form screen follow the procedure above.

Task 5: Printing the Table of Classes form

 To print this form

1   Open the **Table of Classes** form.

2   Click on the **Print Preview** button.

3   Experiment with zooming-in and zooming-out.

4   Use **File-Page Setup** and/or **File-Print** to make adjustments before printing. If no adjustments are necessary, then click on the **Print** button.

5   Close the form.

Customising forms

What you will learn in this unit

Forms are constructed from a collection of individual design elements, which are called *controls*. If you are familiar with Windows applications you will be familiar with dialog boxes and the controls that they contain. The controls that appear on the forms created so far are:

■ labels, so that you know what each part of the form is for

■ text boxes, for entering data.

By the end of this unit you will be able to:

■ display the customising tools (toolbox, palette, properties and field list)

■ move and size controls

■ align controls

■ add text to a form

■ add the date to a form

■ add headers and footers to a printed form.

Customising a form

A form may be modified so that so that it is easier for inexperienced users to enter information into the database. To modify a form you need to display the form in design mode (see following section). AutoForm or Form Wizard is a good way of quickly creating a form. However, the resulting form is rather standardised in terms of vertical spacing between controls, fonts, and colours, so you are likely to want to make modifications.

Components of a form in design view

Component	Function
Form header	Contains text such as the form's title, but field headers and graphics may be put into a header section.
Detail	Contains the controls (field labels, text boxes and check boxes) that display data from the table for which the form has been designed.
Form footer	Similar in function to the form header and may contain information such as the date.

Right margin	The position of the right margin is indicated by a vertical line on the right edge of the form. To move the right margin click and drag the vertical line.
Bottom margin	A horizontal line indicates the bottom margin of the form. This also can be positioned by clicking and dragging.
Scroll bars	Vertical and horizontal scroll bars enable you to move the form within its window.

If you have used a Form Wizard to create the form, only the header band and the detail band contain controls. The header band contains information that will always appear at the top of the form, usually the title of the form. The detail band contains the controls for displaying the data.

Form Design View

So far in this series of units you have only opened a form in the Form run (data) View. This is the mode in which forms are usually run, where they display and, more importantly, accept data. A form can also be shown in Design View, which allows modifications to be made to its layout. In Design View data cannot be entered into the form, only the layout and appearance of the form can be changed. A form has a different appearance in Design View, as illustrated in FIGURE 14.1.

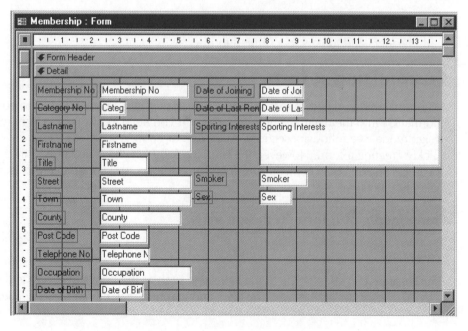

FIGURE 14.1 Membership form shown in Design View

Instead of data appearing in the controls, the field names appear. Text or controls may be selected and moved to achieve the layout desired.

Label and text box controls

A field usually has two controls: a label control in which the field name appears and a text box control in which the data will appear when the form is run.

Extra windows

Other features of design view are:

■ availability of rulers and grid

■ design aids in the form of other small windows:

　■ the Toolbox

　■ the Field List

　■ the Properties Sheet.

 The Toolbox offers a selection of tools by which controls and text may be added to the form. The Field List shows a list of fields in the table that the form was based upon and the Properties sheet is a list of properties. These will depend upon what part of the form is selected. You will become familiar with these as you progress through the tasks. To display the Toolbox click on the **Toolbox** button or use **View-Toolbox**. To display the Field List click on the **Field List** button or choose **View-Field List**. To display the Properties sheet click on the **Properties** button on the toolbar or choose **View-Properties**.

The buttons above are (from left to right) the **Field List** button, the **Toolbox** button and the **Properties** button.

Colour selection

 Colour selection can be made using the drop down buttons on the formatting tool-bar. These will be considered in Unit 22.

Opening a form in design view

1　From the database window, click on the **Forms** tab.

2　Select the name of the form required and click on the **Design** button.

Once a form is open you may switch between the Form run (data) View and the Design View by clicking on the **View** button on the toolbar.

Run form  Design form

Moving and sizing controls

Before you can move or size a control you must select it by clicking anywhere on its surface. When selected, the control is enclosed by an outlining rectangle with an anchor rectangle at its upper left corner and seven smaller rectangles. These smaller rectangles are sizing handles. On columnar forms text boxes often have associated labels and when you select one of these objects they are selected together as a unit.

To	Do this
Select a text box control and its label (if it has a label)	Click anywhere on either the label or the text box.
Move a text box control and its label (if it has a label)	After selecting, move the pointer over the label until it changes shape to a hand. Click and drag the label and box to new position.
Move label or text box control separately	After selecting, move the pointer over the anchor handle at the top left corner of either the label or text box control. The pointer should change shape to a pointing hand. Click and drag to new position.
Adjust the width and height of a control simultaneously	Move the pointer over one of the small sizing handles at one of the three corners. It should change to a diagonal two-headed arrow. Click and drag to size required.
Adjust only the height of the control	Move the pointer over one of the sizing handles on the horizontal surface of the outline. It should change shape to a vertical two-headed arrow. Click and drag to height required.
Adjust only the width of the control	Move the pointer over one of the sizing handles on the vertical surface of the outline. It should change shape to a horizontal two-headed arrow. Click and drag to width required.

Selecting and moving a group of controls

You can select and move more than one object at a time. This is useful if you want to keep the relative spacing of a group of objects yet want to move them to another part of the form.

To select a group of objects, either:

■ imagine that the group of objects is enclosed by a rectangle. Use the pointer and by clicking and dragging draw this rectangle on the form. When you release the mouse button all the objects within this rectangle will be selected, or

■ select one object, hold down the *Shift* key whilst selecting the next and subsequent objects (this is easier when controls are in close proximity).

To move the whole group, with the pointer as the shape of a hand drag the group to its new position. To move an individual control in the group, point to its anchor handle and drag.

To deselect one object in the group, click on it while holding down the *Shift* key. To deselect the whole group, click anywhere outside the selected area.

Using the ruler and the grid

The View-Ruler command will select whether or not the ruler is displayed. When a control is being dragged, indicator lines slide along both rulers to aid positioning of controls.

View-Grid will display or hide a grid of small dots, which are also an aid to the positioning of controls. The spacing of the grid can be adjusted by altering the setting of the Grid X and Grid Y properties on the form's property sheet. To display the form property sheet, as shown in FIGURE 14.3, use Edit-Select Form and click on the Properties button.

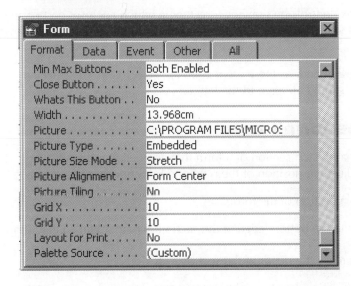

FIGURE 14.2 Form properties sheet

When Format-Snap to Grid is on (indicated by a tick next to Snap to Grid in the menu), any new controls drawn on the form will have their corners aligned to points on the grid. When Snap to Grid is off the control can be placed anywhere.

Aligning a group of controls

Once you start to move controls around the form they can become untidy as they become misaligned. By selecting a group of controls together they can be aligned. Select labels and text boxes separately for alignment purposes.

To align labels.

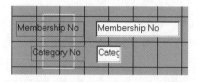 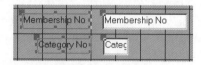

1 Select the labels by drawing a rectangle which encloses part or all of all the labels you wish to select (see above). Alternatively click each label while holding down the *Shift* key.

2 Choose **Format-Align** and, as these are labels, select **Right**. The selected group of controls should all align to the right.

To align text box controls:

1 Select the text box controls by drawing a rectangle which encloses part or all of all the text boxes you wish to select, or click each text box while holding down the *Shift* key.

2 Choose **Format-Align** and, as these are text boxes, select **Left**. The selected group of controls should all align to the left.

Changing the form's area

You can alter the area of each section of a form (header, detail and footer) individually. You can also adjust the position of the right and bottom edges of a form.

To alter the depth of a section of the form:

1 Move the pointer to the bottom edge of the section, where it will change shape.

2 Drag down to increase the depth of the section. ↕

To alter the area of the form drag the right and bottom edges to the size that you require.

Task 1: Customising the Membership form

Open the Chelmer Leisure Membership form in Design View. The aim of this task is to create the form shown in FIGURE 13.1. Exact instructions are not given as you can experiment with selecting and moving controls. You may find it useful to widen the form temporarily so that controls can be moved to temporary positions while you rearrange them on the form. If you wish to keep a group of controls together, select and move them as a group. Also try aligning groups of controls to achieve a tidy looking form.

If you inadvertently delete a field from the form see the following table for instructions on how to restore it. When you have rearranged the detail section, save the form design using **File-Save**.

Deleting or restoring fields from or to a form

To	Do this
Delete a label or label and text box	Select the control and press *Delete* or use **Edit-Delete** to delete both label and entry box. To delete only the label click on it again before deleting.
	If you delete a field, you won't be able to use the form to enter data into this field. Use **Edit-Undo** if you unintentionally delete a field.
Restoring a label and field	Use **View-Field List** to display the list of fields available in the table. Click on the field name required, and drag to the required position on the form. If the form is a single column form then both label and field will appear, although the label will require editing. If the form is a tabular one then just the field will be restored.

Changing the text of a field name label

You can edit the text of a field name label and if required, add text to the form.

To	Do this
Add a label	Click on the **Label** tool in the Toolbox window; click on the form in the required position and type ![Aa] the text required.
Edit a label	Double-click on the label to display an insertion point in the text. Edit the text as required. Press *Enter* or click on a blank part of the form when finished.

Altering the size and font of controls

To alter the size or font of controls in a form:

1   Select the control(s) to be altered.

2   Open the **Font** list box in the toolbar and select the font required.

3   Open the **Point Size** list box and select the point size required.

4   Click on **Left** , **Centre** or **Right** alignment button in the toolbar.

If you increase the size of a font you may need to alter the size of the control and the size of the section.

Task 2: Adding text to the form header

In this task you will add text to the header section of the **Membership** form.

1   Open the **Membership** form in design mode.

2   Widen the Form Header section.

3   Click on the **Label** tool in the Toolbox window.

4   Click in the space created for the form header and key in the text *Chelmer Leisure and Recreation Centre*. Drag the label to make it larger, and increase the size of this text. You may also wish to change the font.

5   Move and size the heading as in FIGURE 14.4, add the text *Membership Application Form*. If you wish you may alter the font or size of this text. Save and close the form.

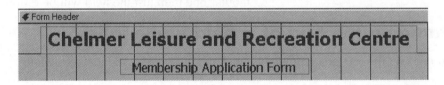

FIGURE 14.3 Heading in the form header

Task 3: Using the customised form to enter data

To gain a full appreciation of the modifications made to the **Membership** form then it should be used to enter data.

1   Open the form from the Database window by clicking on the **Open** button.

2   Move through the records and display a blank form.

3   Compose data for a new member and, using the form, enter data into the next record.

4   Close the form.

Reorganising the field order

When data is entered into each field, *Enter* or *Tab* takes you to the next field. The order in which the fields are entered is defined by the order in which they were selected in the **Form Wizard**. Once the form has been modified then this order may need to be changed.

To change the Tab order of the fields:

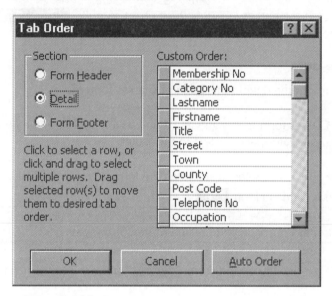

FIGURE 14.4

1   Open the form in design view.

2   Choose **View-Tab Order** to display the **Tab Order** dialog box. This dialog box displays the order of the fields in the **Custom Order** box. In the **Section** box **Detail** is normally selected.

3   To alter the order of the fields select the field or fields to be moved and drag to the new position.

4   When the new order has been selected click on **OK** .

The **Auto Order** button will set the Tab order according to the way in which the fields are set out on the form. They are ordered with the priority of left to right and then top to bottom.

Adding headers and footers

It is straightforward to add text into the header and footer sections of a form. Headers and footers are always displayed on the screen. Calculated text may be added to the header or the footer; for example, the date can be shown.

If a form is to be printed the header section prints before the first record and the footer section prints after the last record. Extra sections - page header and page footer - can be added, which will print on each page of the printout. You can control whether to display or print these sections. Calculated text may be added to show the page numbers.

Page breaks may occur in the middle of records if the record is in single column format. This can be avoided by adjusting the Keep Together setting of the Detail properties from No to Yes. To display the Properties sheet check that the Properties button is depressed and click on the detail bar.

Task 4: Adding the date

The aim of this task is to put the date in the **Table of Classes** form footer.

1 Open the **Table of Classes** form in design view. Point to the bottom of the Form Footer bar and drag to create space for text in the footer.

2 Choose Insert-Date and Time. Select a suitable date format, remove the tick from the time tick box, and click on OK .

3 Drag the Date control to the space you created in the form footer.

4 Switch to run mode by clicking on the Form View button to see the result. Close the form.

Task 5: Adding headers and footers to a printed form

When a form is printed the header is printed at the beginning and the footer is printed at the end of the records. To add a header that prints at the top of each page and a footer that prints at the bottom of each page of the **Membership** form when printed:

1 Open the **Membership** form.

2 Click on the Print Preview button.

3 Close the preview and display the form in design view.

4 Choose View-Page Header/Footer. Two extra sections appear: Page Header and Page Footer.

5   Select all the titles in the form header and use **Edit-Copy**.

6   Click on the Page Header bar and use **Edit-Paste**. Position the pasted copy.

7   Click on the Page Footer bar and choose **Insert-Page Number**. Choose a suitable format and click on **OK**.

8   Click on Form Header bar. Display the Properties sheet by clicking on the **Properties** button on the toolbar.

9   In the **Section properties** box select the **All** tab and click in the **Display When** box.

10 Open the list and select **Screen Only**.

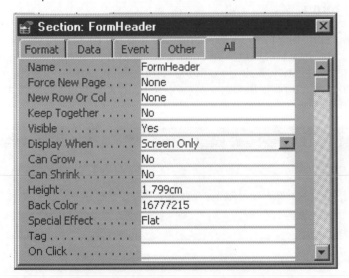

FIGURE 14.5

11 Click on the Detail bar and change the **Keep Together** property to **Yes**, to prevent page breaks in the middle of records.

12 Preview and print the form.

13 Save and close the form.

What you will learn in this unit

This unit reviews and offers practice on the following topics:

- creating and saving forms
- using forms
- printing forms
- customising forms.

Task 1: Creating forms

1   Using Form Wizard create a form for entering data into the **Chelmer Estates Properties** table. Since we will normally enter records as new properties are registered with the estate agency, a single column form, which presents a form for entering one record at a time is the most appropriate. Try creating a form similar to the one shown below.

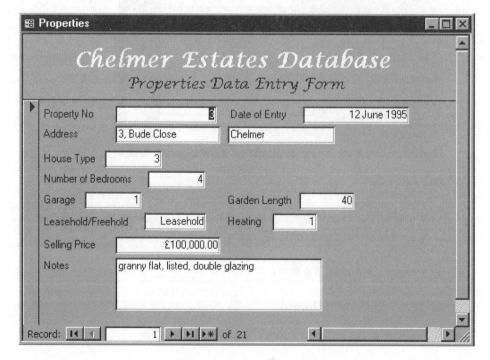

FIGURE 15.1

2   Save the form as **_Properties_**.

Task 2: Using a form

Remember that when a blank form is displayed (ready to accept data for a new record), default values will have already been entered for those fields for which you set default values when you were defining the field properties in the table definition process.

1 Enter two records of your own choice into the **Properties** table using the form **Properties**.

2 Experiment with entering data that contravenes the validation rules and check that these are operating appropriately.

3 You may leave these additional records in the table.

Task 3: Printing from a form

1 Preview the form on screen in order to see how it will look when printed.

2 Print one page of the form printout.

 Remember that forms are intended for screen use, and that if you routinely wish to print a set of records you should use a report (see Unit 16). Printing of forms is most useful for examining screen design.

Task 4: Changing a form's control

In this optional task we will consider changing the control for the **Yes/No** (**Leasehold/Freehold**) field from a text box to a check box control.

1 Open the form **Properties** in design view.

2 Delete the control for **Leasehold/Freehold**.

3 Display the **Field List** by clicking on the **Field List** button or using View-Field List. Similarly display the **Toolbox**.

4 Click on the check box button in the **Toolbox** and then click and drag the **Leasehold/Freehold** field on to the form into its previous position. Adjust its position and save the form as *Properties2*.

5 Try this and the **Properties** form for entering data to see the difference between the two types of control.

Reports

What you will learn in this unit

This unit explores the basic design of printed reports that include data from an Access table. It explains how to create a report quickly using Report Wizard. Later units develop some of the themes in this unit more fully.

By the end of this unit you will be able to:

- create a report using Report Wizard or AutoReport

- save and close a report

- use a report to print data from an Access table.

Printing data and information

Reports are used to print information from a number of records. Reports can show the data from either a table or a query. In addition to records, they may show summary information relating to the records displayed.

Reports, then, are intended to allow you to select the data to be printed and then to present that data in an acceptable format. To emphasise the distinction between reports and forms: reports are intended to be printed, screen forms are normally displayed on screen, although the facilities also often exist for printing them.

In most applications you will create a number of different standard reports. For example, a mailing list of clients may simply show customer name and address, but a list showing outstanding orders to specific clients will include details of the items customers have ordered, their value and other associated information.

Access allows you to create reports to your own design using its wide range of tools for customising reports, or to start by using Report Wizard, which provides you quickly and easily with a basic report, which you can later format and customise. We use Report Wizards here because they allow you to understand the basic concepts of what a report is and how it works, before you grapple with customising specific features of the report.

Since forms and reports share many design and creation features, you will re-use some of the skills that you acquired earlier in designing a form to help you to design a report.

Creating a single column report with a Report Wizard

(d.) There are various types of report that can be created with a Report Wizard. First we deal with the single column report, which is used most frequently and is relatively simple to create. A single column report places all the selected fields in a single column, with their field names to the left as shown in FIGURE 16.4.

To enter Report Wizard starting from the Database window.

1 Click on New in the Database window when you are displaying reports, or click the New Object button on the toolbar and select Report. A New Report dialog box appears.

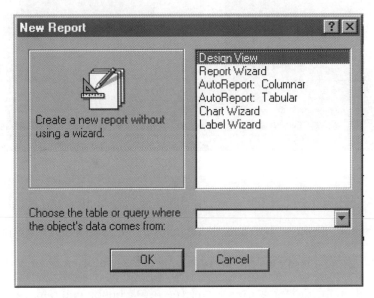

FIGURE 16.1

2 Select the Report Wizard option to create a report using Report Wizard.

3 Click on the Down Arrow button of the Choose a table or query.. list box, to produce a list of tables and queries and select the table for which you wish to create a report.

4 Click on OK .

5 The next stage is to choose which fields are to be in the report. The fields that you can have in the report are shown in the Available Fields box.

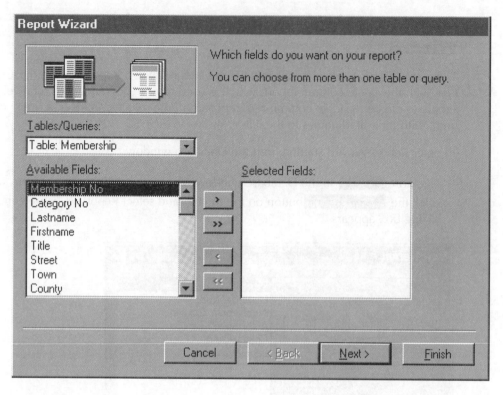

FIGURE 16.2

6 Transfer the fields required to the report by selecting each in turn and clicking on the ⟩ button. If you wish to add all the fields in the table then click on the ⟩⟩ button. You can set the order in which the fields appear on the report by selecting them in the order that you desire. The ⟨ button will remove a highlighted field and ⟨⟨ will remove all the fields.

7 Once you have added the required fields continue by clicking on the Next > button.

8 The next dialog box asks you to indicate grouping levels. Leave this for now and click on the Next > button. We shall return to this in Unit 17.

9 The next dialog box asks you to select the order in which records will be sorted. Select the fields you want the records to be sorted by. If you have only a small set of records just one sort field will be adequate. If you want records to appear in the same order as in the table or query it is not necessary to indicate a sort field. Choose the Next > button.

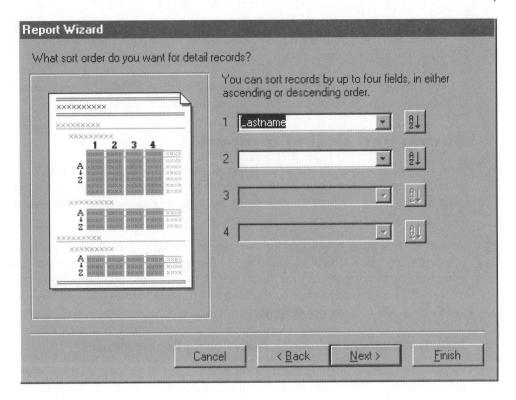

FIGURE 16.3

10 The next dialog box concerns itself with the layout of the printout on the paper and whether the report is to be in portrait or landscape orientation. The choice of layout depends on whether or not grouping is used. On the first occasion choose **Columnar** and **Portrait**. Click on the Next > button.

11 You are then asked what kind of style you want for your form. You are given a choice of:

- Bold
- Casual
- Compact
- Corporate
- Formal
- Soft Gray

The style decides the appearance of the field names and field contents in the report. An example of the style is shown on the left of the dialog box. Click on each style in turn to see what it would look like. On the first occasion a report is created choose **Corporate**. The style can be modified later. Click on the Next > button.

12 Next you are asked for a title; enter a report title. Report titles are particularly important in flagging the purpose of the report to the reader, so choose something that conveys the contents.

13 With the option **Preview the report** selected, click on **Finish**. Note that Access has added a page number and the date at the bottom of every page.

Saving and closing a report

Save a report by choosing **File-Save**. If this is a new report that does not have a name, Access will prompt for a file name with a **File-Save As** dialog box. If you later want to save a report under another name use **File-Save As**, and enter the new name in the dialog box.

Remember that there is a distinction between the name and the title of a report. The title is the text that is displayed at the top of the report when it is printed. The name you give when saving the form is the form's file name, which you need to be able to recognise when you want to open the form again. These names appear in the Database window when the **Report** tab is selected.

Task 1: Creating a columnar report using Report Wizard

We wish to create a single column report that lists the records for all the Chelmer Leisure members who have records in the database, showing the following fields:

■ Membership No

■ Category No

■ Firstname

■ Lastname

■ Occupation

■ Date of Birth

■ Sporting Interests.

We wish to create a report that looks like the extract shown in FIGURE 16.4.

Chelmer Leisure and Recreation Centre Members

Membership No	1
Category No	2
Firstname	Andrew J
Lastname	Walker
Occupation	Builder
Date of birth	12/3/52
Sporting Interests	Tennis, squash
Membership No	2
Category No	1
Firstname	Denise
Lastname	Cartwright

FIGURE 16.4 The beginning of a single column report

1 To enter Report Wizard, starting from the Database window click on **New** when you are displaying reports, or click the **New Object** button on the toolbar and select **New Report**. A **New Report** dialog box appears.

2 Select the **Report Wizard** option.

3 Click on the **Down Arrow** button of the **Choose the table or query..** list box, to produce a list of tables and queries, and select the **Membership** table. Click on **OK**.

4 Select the fields to appear in the report by clicking on the field names above in the **Available Fields** list box, and then clicking on the **>** button. The selected fields should appear in the **Selected Fields** list box. If any fields are included by mistake, use **<** to remove them. Choose **Next >**.

5 Do not indicate a grouping level; if Access has automatically created one (on Category No) then click on **<** to remove the grouping. Click on the **Next >** button.

6   Choose to sort by Membership No by selecting it from the first drop-down list box. Click on the Next > button.

7   Choose columnar and portrait for the layout of the report. Click on the Next > button.

8   Choose Corporate for the Style of the report. Click on the Next > button.

9   Enter the following report title: *Chelmer Leisure and Recreation Centre Members*.

10 With the option **Preview the report** selected, click on Finish to display the report on the screen. Access will automatically save the report with the name **Chelmer Leisure and Recreation Centre Members**.

11 Close the report.

Using a report

To use a report, first display the available report names in the Database window, then double click on the report name and the Print Preview window will appear showing a preview of how the report will appear when printed. Alternatively, click on the report name and then click on the Preview button.

To zoom in and out and to view a complete page on the screen, click on the report.

Note that a report picks up the table properties of the table or query the report uses when it was designed. Later, you will change the properties of the table or query without changing the properties of the report.

Printing a report

Before printing any report always view the report in Print Preview.

Previewing

To preview a report:

1   Click the Preview button, and a miniature version of what is to be printed will be displayed. 🔍

2   To zoom-in and zoom-out simply click anywhere on the preview, or use the Zoom button. Click on the **Zoom Control** box to select a specific magnification for the preview.

3   Choose **File-Page Setup** to make adjustments such as the orientation (portrait or landscape), the choice of printer and the width of the margins. Some of the

options in the Page Setup dialog box will be familiar since you will have used them in printing tables and queries, but there are also special options for use when printing reports, such as the number of columns across the page and their size. Click on ▮OK▮ when the required adjustments have been made.

Printing

When you are satisfied that the preview is correct, you can print from either the preview screen or the design screen.

To print from the preview screen.

1 Click on the ▮Print▮ button in the print preview bar.

2 Select whether all or certain pages of the report will be printed and the number of copies. Click on ▮OK▮.

To print from the design screen, choose File-Print and follow step 2 above.

Task 2: Using and printing a report

1 To use the report **Chelmer Leisure and Recreation Centre Members**, first select it from the file names displayed in the Database window, by double clicking on the report name. The Print Preview window will appear showing a preview of how the report will appear when printed.

2 Choose File-Page Setup.

3 Experiment with different Setup options, for example:

   ■ Have two columns across the page by entering *2* in the Number of Columns Across box. Change the page orientation to landscape and you may need to adjust the Width in the Column Size section to less than half your page width.

   ■ With two columns on the page explore the effect of Down, then Across and Across, then Down in the Column layout section.

   ■ Try increasing the capital Height in the Column Size section.

   Close the Print Setup dialog box between each trial in order to view the new layout in Print Preview.

4 When you have a layout with which you are happy, print it, by selecting the ▮Print▮ button, followed by ▮OK▮.

Creating a report using AutoReport

The really easy way to create a report is to allow Access to do all the work for you by using AutoReport. This, however, does not allow any scope for specifying the report's contents or style.

To use AutoReport.

1 Click on **Reports** and the **New** button.

2 In the New Report dialog box select either AutoReport: Columnar or AutoReport: Tabular.

3 Click on the down arrow button of the Choose a table or query.. list box, to produce a list of tables and queries and select the table for which you wish to create a report.

4 Click on **OK** and the report will be created and displayed on the screen.

5 Use File-Save and give the report a name.

Task 3: Creating a tabular report using AutoReport

1 Click on **Reports** and the **New** button.

2 In the New Report dialog box select either AutoReport: Tabular or AutoReport: Columnar.

3 Click on the down arrow button of the Choose a table or query.. list box, and select the table Classes.

4 Click on **OK** and the report will be created and displayed on the screen in preview mode.

5 Save it as ***Table of Classes*** and print this report.

Grouped reports

What you will learn in this unit

This unit explores the creation of reports where records are arranged in groups according to the value of fields in a table or query.

By the end of this unit you will be able to:

■ create a report with grouped records.

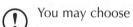 You may choose to omit this unit for the moment and return to it later.

Understanding grouped reports

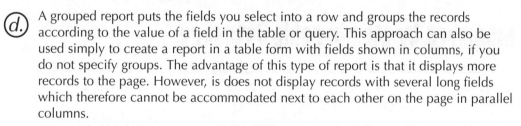 A grouped report puts the fields you select into a row and groups the records according to the value of a field in the table or query. This approach can also be used simply to create a report in a table form with fields shown in columns, if you do not specify groups. The advantage of this type of report is that it displays more records to the page. However, is does not display records with several long fields which therefore cannot be accommodated next to each other on the page in parallel columns.

Records can be grouped by several different fields, although we shall use only one field for grouping.

Apart from the need to define how records will be displayed in groups, the process of creating a groups/totals report is similar to that for a single column report. The process is basically the following steps:

1 Select the fields to appear in the report.

2 Select how the records in the table or query will be grouped for the report. Groups are divisions within a report that include all records that have a value for a specific field.

3 Select the order in which you want the groups created (if you are using more than one group).

4 Select how the records are to be sorted for the report.

5 Select a layout for the report.

6 Select a style for the report.

7 Add the report's title.

8 Select Print Preview to display the report on screen.

9 Save the report.

10 Print the report, as appropriate, and subsequently, close the report.

Task 1: Creating a grouped report using Report Wizard

We wish to create a grouped report that lists all the members for whom there are records in the Chelmer Leisure database, showing the following fields:

- **Category No**
- **Lastname**
- **Firstname**
- **Telephone No**

The records are to be grouped according to Category No, so that, for instance, all records with a given Category No are grouped together. We wish to create a report that looks like the one shown in FIGURE 17.1.

Members by Membership Category

Category No	Lastname	Firstname	Telephone No
1			
	Barrett	Martha A	01777 557822
	Cartwright	Denise	01777 552099
	Davies	Sandra M	01778 891441
	Jameson	Donna	
	Jones	Edward R	01777 567333
	Robinson	Rebecca	01777 568812
	Weiner	George W F	
2			
	Everett	Alan	
	Forsythe	Ann M	01777 569945
	Shangali	Imran	01777 561553

FIGURE 17.1 An extract from a group/totals report created using Report Wizard

1 Open the **Chelmer Leisure** database.

2 Enter Report Wizard by clicking the `New` button in the Database window with the `Reports` tab selected.

3 Click on the Report Wizard option.

4 From the **Choose a table or query..** drop down list box select the **Membership** table. Click on **OK** .

5 Select the fields to appear in the report by clicking on the fields names as indi-cated above, in the **Available Fields** list box, and then clicking on the **>** button. The selected fields should appear in the **Selected Fields** list box. If any fields are included by mistake use **<** to remove them.

6 Click on **Next >** . To group by Category No click on **Category No** in the list of fields and then click on **>** to display it in the heading box in the preview. If Access has automatically grouped the records by Category No then accept this.

7 Click on **Next >** .

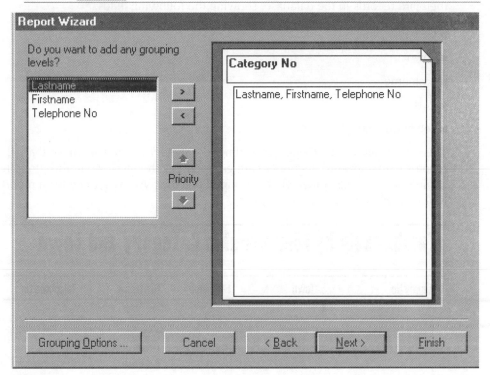

FIGURE 17.2

8 Sort records within groups alphabetically by the **Lastname** field. Click on **Next >** .

9 Select **Stepped** and **Portrait** for the layout of the report. Click on **Next >** .

10 Select **Compact** for the style of the report. Click on ▌Next >▐ .

11 Enter the following report title: ***Members by Membership Category***.

12 Choose **Preview the report** and click on ▌**Finish**▐ . Since the wizard was used to create the report it is automatically saved with the name of its title, i.e. **Members by Membership Category**.

13 To print the report directly, click on the ▌**Print**▐ button. To change print options display the **Print** dialog box using **File-Print** and make the choices you require before clicking on ▌**OK**▐ .

Task 2: Creating a grouped report using more than one group

In this task you will create a grouped report which lists all the members for which there are records in the database, showing the following fields:

- Category No
- Town
- Lastname
- Firstname
- Telephone No

The records are to be grouped according to Category No and Town, so that all records with a given Category No are grouped together and within this grouping all records with a given Town will be grouped together. We wish to create a report that looks like the one shown in FIGURE 17.3.

Membership by Membership Category and Town

Category No	Town	Lastname	Firstname	Telephone No
1				
	Chelmer			
		Jameson	Donna	
		Jones	Edward R	01777 567333
		Robinson	Rebecca	01777 568812
		Weiner	George W F	
	Meirton			
		Barrett	Martha A	01777 557822
		Cartwright	Denise	01777 552099
		Davies	Sandra M	01778 891441

FIGURE 17.3   An extract from a group/totals report created using two levels of grouping

1   Follow the first six steps as for the previous task. To group the records by

   Category No click on Category No in the list of fields and then click on $\boxed{>}$ to
   display it in the heading box in the preview.

2   To add Town to the grouping select it and click on the $\boxed{>}$ button. Click on
   $\boxed{\text{Next >}}$.

3   Sort records within groups alphabetically by the **Lastname** field. Click on
   $\boxed{\text{Next >}}$.

4   Select Stepped and Portrait for the layout of the report. Choose $\boxed{\text{Next >}}$.

5   Select Compact for the style of the report. Choose $\boxed{\text{Next >}}$.

6   Enter the following report title: *Members by Membership Category and Town.*

7   Choose Preview the report and click on $\boxed{\text{Finish}}$.

8   As the wizard was used to create the report it is automatically saved with the
   name of its title, i.e. **Members by Membership Category and Town**. To print the
   report directly, click on the $\boxed{\text{Print}}$ button. To change print options display the
   Print dialog box using File-Print and make the choices you require before clicking on $\boxed{\text{OK}}$.

Task 3: Selecting the order of grouping

Create a report, which is the same as the one in the previous task, but with the
records grouped according to Category No and Town. This time show all records
with a given Town grouped together and within this grouping show all records with
a given Category No grouped together. Create this report as the last task and when
you have added Town as a grouping, click on the $\boxed{\text{Priority}}$ up arrow to change the
priority of grouping. Continue as before but title this report *Members by Town and
Membership Category* and note the difference between this report and the last.

Mailing label reports

What you will learn in this unit

Mailing label reports allow the creation of mailing labels from, say, a table of names and addresses. A mailing label report fits the fields you select into a rectangle that is designed to print labels. Unlike other Report Wizard reports this type does not show field names. It does, however, make it easy to add text such as commas and spaces.

By the end of this unit you will be able to:

- create a mailing label report

- use a query in the process of creating a Report Wizard report

- perform a mail merge to create an accompanying letter.

Creating a mailing label report

The procedure for creating a mailing label report is similar to that for creating any other type of report, except that you use a special Label Wizard.

To create a mailing label report:

1   With the **Reports** tab of the Database window selected, click on **New** .

2   Click on the **Label Wizard** option and select a table or query to provide the data for the labels report. Click on **OK** to display the first of the **Label Wizard** dialog boxes.

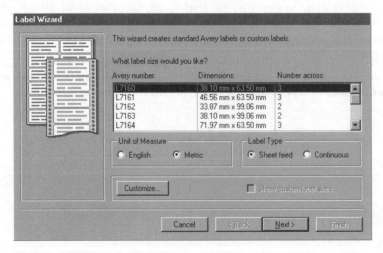

FIGURE 18.1

3   Select the size of labels from the list. Label sizes are listed according to their Avery number. If you do not know the Avery label number for a given label size, look at the Dimensions and Number across columns to find the label size that matches your labels.

4   Select Unit of **Measure** and **Label Type** and click on **Next >** .

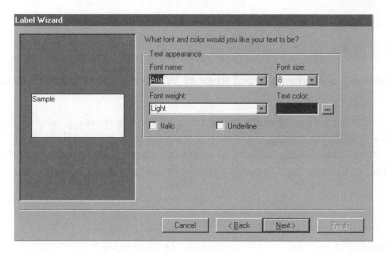

FIGURE 18.2

5   Select the **Font name**, **Font size**, **Font weight** and **Text colour**. You may also check **Italic** and/or **Underline**. Click on the **Next >** button.

6   Select fields as with other report types, so that they appear on the prototype label but remembering that more than one field can be added to a line.

7   Add text, fields and punctuation to a line and then advance to a new line by pressing *Enter*. When you have created the label, click on the **Next >** button.

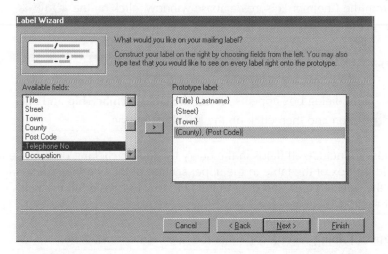

FIGURE 18.3

111

8   Select how the records are to be sorted, or in other words the order in which mailing labels are to be printed. Click on the Next > button.

9   Either accept the name for the report or type in a name for the report. With **See the mailing labels as they will look printed** selected click on Finish to display labels on screen.

10 Save the report.

11 Print and close the report as appropriate.

Task 1: Creating a mailing label Report Wizard report based on a query

We wish to create a mailing label report that lists all members who joined in the last year, i.e. since 1/1/96. An extract from such a report is shown in FIGURE 18.4. First we need to define and execute a query to select the appropriate records, and then we need to define the mailing label report that is to be used to display this set of records.

Mr Gray
4 The Parade
Chelmer
Cheshire, CH1 7ER

Miss Robinson
16 Lowton Lane
Branford
Staffs, ST10 2DZ

FIGURE 18.4 An extract from a mailing label report created using Label Wizard

Query design and execution were introduced earlier, and you may wish to review this topic at this point.

1   Starting from the Chelmer Leisure database window, click on the Queries tab, and click on the New button to create a new query.

2   Choose **Design View** and click on OK .

3   The **Show Table** dialog box appears. Select the table **Membership** and click on the Add button and then click on the Close button.

4   Next choose to include all fields in the query by double clicking on the title bar of the field list box of the table in the upper section of the window. Click anywhere in the selected area and drag to the field row to transfer all the fields to the lower section.

5   In the **Date of Joining** criteria cell enter the query criteria *>1/1/96*.

6 To view the result of this query click on the ▐ Query View ▐ button on the toolbar.

7 Save the query by choosing **File-Save**.

8 In the **Query Name** box of the **Save As** dialog box, enter the Query Name: *New Members*. Click on ▐ OK ▐.

9 Close the query.   Now that you have defined a query, you need to design a report to display the records retrieved by the query.

10 Click on the ▐ Reports ▐ tab in the Database window and click on ▐ New ▐.

11 Select the **Label Wizard** option to create a report using Label Wizard.

12 From the **Choose the table or query..** drop down list box select the query **New Members**. Click on ▐ OK ▐.

13 Select the size of the labels. You may need to experiment with different label sizes. Try the Avery number at the top of the list first. Click on the ▐ Next > ▐ button.

14 Leave the font as default and click on the ▐ Next > ▐ button.

15 Add the field **Title** followed by a space and then the field **Lastname** to the first line. Press *Enter* to move onto the next line.

16 Add **Street** to the next line.

17 Add the remainder of the fields, each to a separate line, with the exception of **County** and **Post Code**, which should be on the same line separated by a comma and a space. Click on the ▐ Next > ▐ button.

18 Choose to order the records in alphabetical order according to **Lastname**. Click on the ▐ Next > ▐ button.

19 Accept the title **Labels New Members**. The report is automatically saved.

20 With **See the labels as they will look printed** selected, click on ▐ Finish ▐ to display the report on the screen.

21 To print the report directly select the ▐ Print ▐ button. To display the **Print** dialog box use **File-Print**.

Customising a report

What you will learn in this unit

This unit explores some of the basic tools for designing customised reports instead of using the standard reports that can be created using Report Wizard.

By the end of this unit you will be able to:

- appreciate the component parts of a report
- create a blank report as a basis for later design work
- move and size controls
- change a report's area
- delete, add and restore fields to a report
- change the text of a field name
- add headers and footers.

Understanding customised reports

Although Report Wizard produces a useful basic report, eventually you may wish to create your own report from scratch, so that you can exercise greater control over the report design. If you examine the Report Wizard reports that you have created recently you will note they have the following limitations: the title length is restricted; the fixed horizontal spacing makes it difficult to distinguish between records; and the fixed format gives the same standard appearance time and time again.

This unit explores some of the simple tools for customising a report. These may be applied either to a report created initially with Report Wizards, or be used to create your own report independently. Before attempting to create or modify a report it is useful to identify the components of a report. These are listed and described below. If you examine the reports you have just created using Report Wizards, you should recognise that they have these components. If you display an existing report in Design View by clicking on the **Design** button with the report selected in the Database window, the report will be displayed with these areas clearly marked.

Components of a report

Component	Function
Component	*Function*
Report Header	Contains any headings or other introductory text that might appear at the beginning of the report.

Page Header	Contains headings that will appear at the top of each page, such as a running title and page numbers.
Detail	Shows data from the records in the database. Sets up the format for records in general, which is then used for every record to be included in the report.
Page Footer	Appears at the bottom of each page.
Report Footer	Contains information at the end of the report, such as a final summary or a statement such as; 'this is the end of the report'.
Group Header	Marks the beginning of a group; usually introduces the group that the report will display.
Group Footer	Marks the end of a group and often contains sections that summarise the records that are part of a group.

Working with report design allows you to adjust the contents, size and position of everything that appears on the report. As with forms, each small piece of a report is called a control. Controls include a field's data, text, picture and calculations. Again, many of the features relating to forms that you experimented with earlier also apply to reports.

Modifying an existing report

To customise an existing report it must be opened in Design View. Either select the report in the Database window and then select the **Design** button, or click on the report name using the right mouse button and choose **Design** from the shortcut menu.

Creating a new blank report

To create a new report, without the aid of Report Wizard:

1   Use one of the following methods to create a new report:

- Click on the **Reports** tab in the Database window and on **New** ; or

- Choose **View-Database Objects-Reports** and then click on the **New** button in the Database window; or

- Click on the drop down **New Object** button on the toolbar, then select **Report**.

2   Select the **Design View** option to create a report without using Report Wizard.

3   Click on the **Down Arrow** button of the **Choose the table or query..** list box, to produce a list of tables and queries and select the table for which you wish to create a report.

4 Click on OK .

Extra windows

When you create a new blank report the Toolbox window will be displayed. This is useful for adding controls to the report. There are a number of such windows that you will encounter as you advance in report design, but they should be familiar as you have met them in form design. These are:

■ **Properties sheet** to change different features of the report's contents

■ **Field list** to add controls bound to fields

■ **Toolbox** to select the design tool required (can be dragged to the left of screen where it 'locks' as a toolbar)

You can move and close any of these windows in the same way as any other window. They can also be opened and closed from the View menu.

Task 1: Examining the components of a report

Examine the report **Members by Membership Category** created with Report Wizard in Unit 17. With the Database window displayed, click on Reports , select this report, and then click on Design . Note that Report Wizards creates reports with default settings in many areas of the report. Examine the report that you have displayed. Click on each control in turn. What are the default settings for:

■ Report Header?

■ Page Header?

■ Group Header?

■ Detail?

■ Group Footer?

■ Page Footer?

■ Report Footer?

Task 2: Creating a blank report

Create a blank report for the **Classes** table, showing all the fields in the table.

1 Click on the Reports tab in the Database window, and then click the New button in the Database window. Select the **Classes** table from the Choose the table or query.. drop down list box. Click on OK .

2 Select the Design View option.

3 Display the field list by choosing View-Field List.

4 Add all the fields to the report from the field list. Double-click on the Field List title bar to highlight all the fields.

5   Click and drag the highlighted fields onto the Detail section of the report. Controls for all the fields should appear.

6   Save as **Classes** and close. You will open this report later to modify its layout.

Moving and sizing controls

Moving and sizing controls is the basic activity for improving the appearance of the report.

In order to move a control, the control must first be selected and then it can be moved by dragging. The different types of controls can be selected in the same way as controls are selected and moved on forms. If you need a reminder, see Moving and sizing controls in Unit 14.

Task 3: Moving and sizing controls on a Report Wizards report

We wish to improve on the design of the report **Chelmer Leisure and Recreation Centre Members**, so that the final report that you will save as **Members2** looks as shown in FIGURE 19.1.

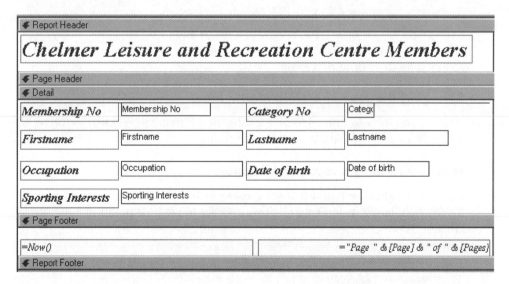

FIGURE 19.1 Design Screen for Members2

1   First open the existing report. Select the report **Chelmer Leisure and Recreation Centre Members** in the Database window and then click on the Design button.

2   Move the controls on the report until it resembles the Design screen in FIGURE 19.1, using the instructions above for selecting and moving controls. If the Toolbox is in the way, remove it by using View-Toolbox. You may get into a muddle in your first attempt to move controls. Remember that controls can be

deleted by selecting them and using the *Delete* key. If all else fails close *without saving* and start again.

3   View the new report on screen using Print Preview.

4   Save the report as **Members2** using **File-Save As**. Close the report.

Customising a report

Changing the report's area

The area of each section of a report (the header, detail and footer sections) may be adjusted. To alter the depth of a section of the form, move the pointer to the bottom edge of the section, where it will change shape. Drag the pointer down to make the section larger, up to make it smaller.

To alter the area of the report drag the right and bottom edges to the size that you require.

Deleting, adding and restoring fields to and from a report

When you create a report from scratch it is necessary to add appropriate fields from a selected table or query. You may also wish to add or delete fields when changing an existing report. Again, procedures are similar to those for deleting, adding and restoring fields to or from a form.

Changing the text of a Field Name label

You can edit the text of a Field Name label and if required add text to the report. Again procedures are similar to those for forms.

Task 4: Creating a customised report

We wish to open the report that we created in Task 2, **Classes**, and move fields and modify field labels as indicated below, in order to create a report like the one in FIGURE 19.2.

1   Open the report **Classes** by selecting the report in the Database window and clicking the Design button.

2   Click on the fields and their labels and move them into a more satisfactory position. Rearrange them as necessary. You may wish to use **Format-Align-Left** to align a group of controls. (Select them as a group first.)

3   Edit the field label **Class No** so that it reads **Number**, by selecting the field label control, clicking where the text editing is required and modifying the field name label. Modify other labels as necessary in the same way.

4   Press *Enter* or click on another part of the report to complete changes.

5   Try aligning groups of controls to achieve a tidy looking report.

6   Next create a report header and footer by choosing **View-Report Header/Footer** so that a tick is placed beside this option.

7   Create a control box into which you can insert the header text, by displaying the Toolbox and clicking on the **Label** tool. Click in the Report Header band at the point where the text is to begin.   *Aa*

8   Type the following text: ***Chelmer Leisure and Recreation Centre - Sports, Fitness and Exercise Classes***.

9   Repeat these steps to insert the text ***Classes*** in the Page Header band.

10 Choose **Insert-Page Numbers** and select **Page N** format and choose the **Bottom of Page (Footer)** option. Leave alignment as Centre and **Show Number on First Page** ticked. Click on **OK** .

11 Adjust the depths of the bands, print preview the report, save the report as Classes and close it.

Chelmer Leisure and Recreation Centre. Sports, Fitness and Exercise Classes

Classes

Number:		1	Class Tutor:	Evans
Class Day:	Monday		Class Activity:	Ladies' Aerobics
Class Time:		10:00	Male/Female/Mixed:	Female
Number:		2	Class Tutor:	Franks
Class Day:	Monday		Class Activity:	Weight Training
Class Time:		11:00	Male/Female/Mixed:	Male

FIGURE 19.2 A customised report

You have now created a basic report showing all the required information, but clearly there is much scope for improvement in its format. Some are explored in the last tasks in this unit, but the majority are the subject of the next few units.

Reformatting a report

Altering the size and font of controls

To alter the size of font of the controls on a report:

1 Select the controls to be altered.

2 Click on the Font list box in the toolbar and select the font required.

3 Click on the Font Size list box and select the point size required.

 If you increase the size of a font you may need to alter the size of the control and the size of the section.

Adding headers and footers

Page headers and footers can be easily added to a report. With the Toolbox displayed click on the **Label** tool. Place the pointer in the appropriate header or footer box and drag it to make a box large enough to accommodate the text.

Task 5: Reformatting a report

This task reformats the report created in the last task, using a number of additional features that have been introduced above.

1 Open the report **Classes** in Design View.

2 Select the controls in the Report Header, open the Font Size list box and select an appropriate larger point size. Click on the **Bold** button to make the text bold. Click on the **Centre** button to centre the text within the control. If necessary stretch the control box to display all the text.

3 Move the field labels into the Page Header band by first selecting them as a group. Choose Edit-Cut and click anywhere in the Page Header. Then choose Edit-Paste.

4 Rearrange the labels in the Page Header to make column headings. Select these as a group and format them by making them bold and italic and of a slightly larger point size.

5 Adjust the size of the Page Header so that it just accommodates the labels by dragging the bottom of the Page Header.

6 In the Detail band, rearrange the controls to align with the labels in the Page Header. If necessary expand the boxes to accommodate the longest field value. For example make sure that the control box for Activity accommodates Badminton.

7 In turn select the text boxes for **Class No** and **Class Time** and left justify them by clicking on the ░▒Align Left▒░ button. Select the **Male/Female/Mixed** control box and delete it by pressing the *Delete* key.

8 Select and format the Report Footer in bold and italics.

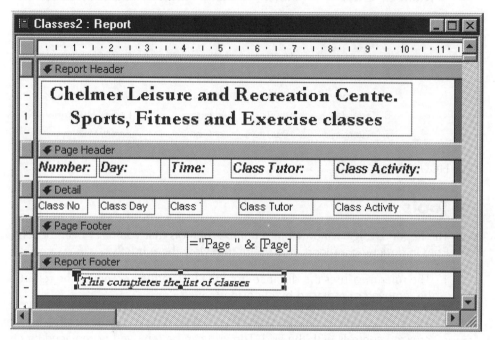

FIGURE 19.3

9 Note that it will probably be necessary to move back and forth between Print preview and Design View a few times as you make changes and want to view the results of those changes.

10 Save as *Classes2*, view using Print Preview, and print as required. Close the report.

Chelmer Leisure and Recreation Centre. Sports, Fitness and Exercise classes

Number:	Day:	Time:	Class Tutor:	Class Activity:
1	Monday	10:00	Evans	Ladies' Aerobics
2	Monday	11:00	Franks	Weight Training
3	Monday	15:00	Latham	Body Conditioning
4	Monday	19:00	Wheildon	Step Aerobics
5	Tuesday	10:00	Jackson	Men's Multi-gym
6	Tuesday	14:00	Adams	Ladies' Multi-gym
7	Tuesday	19:00	Jackson	Family Multi-gym

FIGURE 19.4

Tools

The Report Design window has a number of tools that you have been benefiting from in designing a report. It is useful to review these briefly.

1 The ruler measures the distance from the top and left corner of the report. It can be removed or replaced by choosing **View-Ruler**.

2 The grid appears in Design View. If activated, Access automatically aligns moved or sized controls with the grid. The grid can be removed or replaced by choosing **View-Grid**. To deactivate the grid choose **Format-Snap to Grid**.

3 The align option. Use **Format-Align** to position controls relative to each other. Select the controls you want to align, choose **Format-Align** and select the appropriate alignment, e.g. left.

Consolidating report design

Use the following tasks to practise the report creation skills you have gained from this and the last three units.

Task 6: Creating a single column report using Report Wizard

You require a report, based on the **Membership** table, which lists the following details for all members who are smokers:

■ Membership No

■ Category No

■ Title

■ Firstname

■ Lastname

■ Occupation

■ Date of Birth

■ Sex.

First define a query which allows you to select the records for the members who are smokers. Save this query and then use it in the design of a report using Report Wizard. Don't forget to save the report, as **Smokers**, and print preview it on screen before printing it.

Task 7: Creating a groups/totals report using Report Wizard

You wish to create a report that lists all the classes offered by the centre, based on the **Classes** table. The report is to be organised in groups according to class activity. Include all fields in the **Classes** table.

Produce a second Groups/Totals report, based on the **Classes** table, which details all the information in the **Classes** table. Sort the report in classes order. Save this report as **Classes List**.

Task 8: Creating a customised report

Instead of using Report Wizard to create the report in Task 6, attempt to create the same report independently of the Report Wizards tool, i.e. as a customised report.

Adding lines and rectangles

What you will learn in this unit

This unit is the first of a series that focus on features that allow you to adjust the appearance of the information in reports or forms, and make their presentation more exciting. Access offers a wide range of tools for formatting both screens and reports and supports the imaginative creation of interesting screens and reports. Whilst all these features can be applied to both forms and reports, some are used more often with forms and others are used more often with reports.

By the end of this unit you will be able to:

■ add lines and boxes to forms and reports.

Understanding design

These units focus on those tools concerned with screen and report design. You will already have used some of these features briefly in the last few units. Forms and reports created using Wizards use some of these features to a limited extent, but by the time you have completed these units you should be able to improve on Wizard designs.

Although the tools we explore in these units allow you to be very adventurous with your designs, remember that good design hinges on the appropriate and sparing use of objects such as boxes and lines and on the use of only a limited number of different fonts. In addition most organisations will wish to establish a house style which might be applied to all screens and groups of similar reports. We are not this consistent in the forms and reports that we generate in these units, because the range has been used to demonstrate the wide variety of features and designs that can be adopted. However, when you do need to create a house style, the tips below act as a reminder of good design features.

Design tips - forms

■ Keep the form simple and easy to read. Don't use unnecessary text and graphics, but do use fonts and font sizes that are easy to read on the screen.

■ Use colour sparingly, to make forms interesting, but choose colours that are comfortable for those working at the screen for a long period.

■ Design the form taking into account how it will be used, i.e. where data needs to be entered and ease of movement between data entry boxes.

■ Maintain a consistent appearance for related forms. This looks more professional and makes it easier for a user to acclimatise to a series of forms.

Design tips - reports

■ Keep the report simple. Make the data easy to read by choosing font sizes and types that print well. Use fonts and graphics to help convey important messages in the report.

■ Design in the knowledge of the capabilities of the printer. In particular, colour printers can produce much more intricate detail than non-colour printers.

■ Consider the application of the report. Who are the readers and why will they be using the report?

Adding lines and rectangles to forms and reports

Lines and rectangles can be added to reports and forms to emphasise portions of the form or report or to separate one part from another.

To add lines:

1   Select the **Line** tool in the Toolbox.

2   Point to where you want the line to start.

3   Drag the pointer. The **Line** tool draws a line from where you start dragging the pointer to where you release the mouse.

To add rectangles:

1   Select the **Rectangle** tool in the Toolbox.

2   Point to where you want the corner of the rectangle to be.

3   Drag the pointer to where you want the opposite corner to be.

Changing control layers

When you add boxes to a form or report, they are initially placed on top of any other controls, but as their default fill is transparent any controls already on the form or report that are bounded by the rectangle will still be visible.

 If you want a fill for the rectangle (see Unit 22) then a filled rectangle will cover existing controls. In order to display controls that have been covered, you can take one control and put it behind another. For example, you may move controls hidden by a filled rectangle so that they are on top of the rectangle.

1   To move a control from the front to behind other controls, select it and choose **Format-Send to Back**.

2   To move a control from behind other controls and put it on top, choose **Format-Bring to Front**.

Task 1: Adding lines and rectangles

In this task you will add lines and rectangles to the form **Classes** (created in Task 2 of Unit 13) to make it look similar to FIGURE 20.1.

1   Open the form **Classes** in Design View.

2   Move and size the controls so that they are in the position shown in FIGURE 20.1.

3   Edit the text of the labels appropriately.

4   Place two rectangles around the text in the form header.

5   Select one of the rectangles by clicking on it and practise deleting it by pressing the *Delete* key. You are likely to need to delete lines or boxes that you have placed in the wrong place before you have finished!

6   Recreate the rectangle. Note that if you later choose a fill for either or both these rectangles you need to use **Format-Send to Back** to send the filled rectangle behind the existing controls on the form.

7   Insert a line underneath the controls for Day and Time.

8   Save the form as *Classes3*.

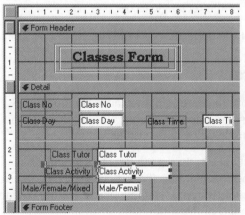
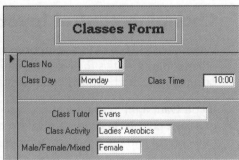

FIGURE 20.1 Form illustrating use of lines and rectangles

Style enhancements

What you will learn in this unit

When in form or report design mode, you may make style enhancements including alignment, colour, three-dimensionality, fonts and borders. These properties are listed in the bottom half of the Property Sheet window and may also be set using buttons on the formatting toolbar. When a control is selected that uses any of the style enhancements described in these units, the middle and right sections of the toolbar change to show the buttons in the table listed below.

By the end of this unit you will be able to:

■ use different alignments

■ use different fonts

■ set dimensions

■ set colours

■ set borders.

Setting alignment and font

This activity explores the use of the formatting toolbar to set alignment and font.

To set alignment or font, select the control to which you wish to add style and then click on an appropriate button. The buttons are described in the table below.

Button	Action
Alignment	
	Aligns text to the left
	Centres text
	Aligns text to the right
Font	
Arial	Font name: sets the style of characters
8	Font size: sets the size of the characters

B   Bold: sets characters as bold

I   Italics: sets characters as italic

U   Underline: underlines characters

Alignment

(d.) Alignment determines whether the characters that appear in the control start at the left side of the control, end at the right side of the control or are centred within the control. The defaults are right alignment for data fields containing numbers and dates and left alignment for all other controls.

It is useful to examine the alignment of controls during the design phase. To do this select the control by clicking on it, and then see which of the alignment buttons is depressed. The most effective alignment depends on how the controls have been arranged on the form or report. For example, in a report showing data in columns with field labels in the Page Header, set the alignment of the headers to the same as that for the entries below them in order to align the headings with the data.

Font

(d.) A font is a collection of features that describes how the text appears. Using two or three different fonts, and using a larger font size or bold or italics can emphasise parts of a report, and make your form or report more interesting.

Although it is possible to set every control to a different font, good design requires you to be selective in the use of fonts. In particular you might consider the following:

■ do not use more than two or three fonts in one report or form

■ select a font that is appropriate for the application; for example, Script and other fancy fonts are not often used in business applications, and where they are used they are used deliberately for effect

■ most, if not all, fonts available to you will be True Type fonts (indicated by a 'two Ts' symbol in the font drop-down list). This depends on the type of printer you have installed. It is best to use True Type fonts when designing a form or report as the printed version will be the same as the screen version

■ Access remembers the printer that is currently selected when you create a form or report and uses fonts specific to the selected printer. If you have a choice of printers then select the correct one in the **Print** dialog box.

Task 1: Setting alignment and fonts on forms

In this task you will set the alignment of the text of the labels, and the font of the text of the labels as shown in FIGURE 21.1.

1   Open the form **Classes3** used in the previous unit.

2 Increase the font size of **Class No**, **Day** and **Time**. You may also need to increase the size of the controls in order to accommodate the text of the labels and the data.

3 Click on each control in turn and check its alignment. Left align controls for all fields except **Class No** which should be right aligned.

4 Save and close the form.

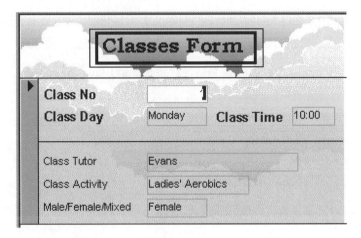

FIGURE 21.1 Setting alignment and fonts on forms

Task 2: Borders, lines, alignment and fonts on reports

The last task involved a form. In this task you are required to apply borders, lines, alignment and fonts to the **Classes** report so that it looks like the one in FIGURE 21.2.

1 Open the **Classes** report created earlier and save it as ***Classes4***.

2 In the Report Header, remove the original text by selecting it and pressing the *Delete* key. Insert two label controls and type in the text shown in FIGURE 21.2. Move the controls to centre them. Centre align the text in the controls. Embolden and enlarge the text and insert a box around it. Use **Format-Send to Back** to redisplay the text.

3 In the Detail band, rearrange the positions of the fields and edit the field names so that they match those shown in FIGURE 21.2.

4 Slightly enlarge the text in the controls and size the controls appropriately.

5 Ensure that all controls are left aligned. To align a group of controls select the group and apply **Format-Align-Left/Right**. Most of these controls are left aligned with respect to each other.

6   Insert a box around the **Class No** controls. Insert a further box to enclose all text in the Detail band.

7   In the Page Header band apply formatting as illustrated to the text Classes. Draw a line underneath it across the width of the form.

8   Insert a line at the top of the Page Footer band.

9   Examine the report in Print Preview, noting especially whether any text is truncated by too small controls.

10 Make any necessary adjustments, Print Preview again, and save the report **Classes4**.

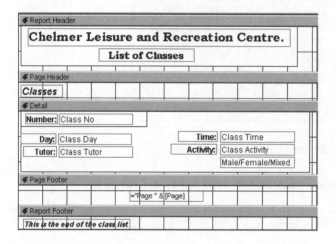

FIGURE 21.2 Form design and printout using borders and fonts

Dimensions, colours and borders

What you will learn in this unit

To make reports and forms look more exciting you can make a control appear three-dimensional, add colour or set borders to different widths. Remember that since most reports are not printed in colour, colours are most likely to be useful for on-screen forms and do not normally need to be set for reports. Equally, three-dimensional controls are particularly useful on forms, where they may be used to highlight labels or to mark out a button.

By the end of this unit you will be able to:

- set dimensions
- set colours
- set borders.

Using the formatting (form/report) toolbar

Special effects, colours and borders can be set using the Formatting (Form/Report) toolbar shown in FIGURE 22.1.

FIGURE 22.1 Formatting toolbar

An alternative way to set these properties is through the Property Sheet window. This can be displayed by double clicking on the control or area whose properties are to be viewed and changed. Generally, it is easier to use the formatting toolbar so we shall restrict ourselves to its use here.

The toolbar's drop-down buttons allow the control of fill/back colour, font/fore colour, line/border colour, line/border width and special effects.

Back, fore and border colours

A control can have separate colours for its background (fill) foreground (font/fore) and border. To set a colour.

1 Select the control.

2 In turn, click on the drop down arrow of the **Fill/back Colour**, **Font/Fore Colour** and **Line/Border Colour** buttons to display the colour selection box, and choose an appropriate colour.

131

3 If you click on the ▓ **Transpart** ▓ button in the colour selection box (Fill/Back and Line/Border), the selected control becomes transparent and is therefore visible, whatever controls are behind it.

Experiment with different colours until you have chosen a colour combination that is legible and draws attention to appropriate parts of the screen.

Line and border widths

All controls have adjustable borders. Some controls, such as the labels for check boxes, option buttons and text boxes, have as a default not to display any border. Others, such as option groups, list boxes and combo boxes, have as a default to display a thin black border.

1 To select a border width click on the drop down arrow of the ▓ **Line/Border Width** ▓ button on the toolbar.

2 From the selection shown choose an appropriate line or border width.

Special effects

You can set the following special effects:

■ flat

■ raised

■ sunken

■ etched

■ shadowed

■ chiselled.

Normal is the default for most controls. To set a special effect:

1 Click on the drop down arrow of the ▓ **Special Effect** ▓ button on the toolbar.

2 From the selection shown choose the effect you want to use.

When you select raised, sunken, etched, shadowed or chiselled the control adopts the same colours as buttons on the toolbar and command buttons to achieve the effect. These colours are set by the Windows Control Panel. It is only possible to change the fore and back colour.

When a control is shown as raised, sunken, etched, shadowed or chiselled changing the border width will cause the control to revert to flat.

Task 1: Setting dimensions and borders

Open the form **Classes3** in Design View and use it to experiment with setting dimensions, colours and borders. For example:

1   Set all the field labels as raised.

2   Set the Form Header as sunken

3   Widen the line in the Detail band

4   Apply some colours to different parts of the screen to add to its visual interest.

Reviewing reports

What you will learn in this unit

This unit reviews and offers practice on the following topics:

■ creating a single column report using Report Wizards

■ using and printing a single column report

■ creating a mailing label report.

Task 1: Creating a single column report using Report Wizard

This task creates a single column report for all of the properties in the **Properties** table, sorted in descending order according to Selling Price.

1   Using Report Wizards, create a report, resembling that shown in FIGURE 23.1, that shows the records for all of the properties in the database, including the following fields:

   ■ Property No

   ■ Address

   ■ Town

   ■ Selling Price

   ■ Date of Entry.

2   Sort the records in descending order according to their selling price.

3   Choose a columnar layout for the report. Save the report as **_Properties_**.

Properties

Selling Price	35000
Property No	10
Address	34, Adelaide Road
Town	Chelmer
Date of Entry	02 January 1996
Selling Price	39000
Property No	20
Address	Flat 4, 346, Chelmer Lane
Town	Chelmer

FIGURE 23.1 Single column Properties report

Task 2: Using and printing a report

1 Select the report **Properties** and view it in preview.

2 Print from the preview screen or the design screen.

3 By choosing File-Page Setup, experiment with two or three columns (**Layout** tab) arranged across a landscape page (**Page** tab) as in FIGURE 23.2.

You may need to reduce the item size and column spacing as well as the margins of the page to fit in three columns.

Properties

Selling Price	35000	Selling Price	39000	Selling Price	45000
Property No	10	Property No	20	Property No	18
Address	34. Adelaide Road	Address	Flat 4, 348, Chelmer Lane	Address	Flat 1, Gracelands
Town	Chelmer	Town	Chelmer	Town	Woodford
Date of Entry	02 January 1996	Date of Entry	29 June 1996	Date of Entry	20 June 1996
Selling Price	45000	Selling Price	50000	Selling Price	55000
Property No	7	Property No	4	Property No	6
Address	16. The Close	Address	56. Bodmin Drive	Address	2. Woodford Road
Town	Branford	Town	Chelmer	Town	Merton
Date of Entry	18 November 1995	Date of Entry	20 September 1995	Date of Entry	21 October 1995
Selling Price	60000	Selling Price	65000	Selling Price	67000
Property No	16	Property No	17	Property No	21
Address	159. Moss Lane	Address	34. The Grove	Address	4. St Paul's Avenue
Town	Chelmer	Town	Chelmer	Town	Chelmer
Date of Entry	03 May 1996	Date of Entry	21 May 1996	Date of Entry	04 July 1996

FIGURE 23.2

Task 3: Creating and using a mailing label report

This task asks you to create and use a mailing label report for a set of records selected from the database using a query. We wish to create a mailing label report that lists all detached properties.

1   Create a query that selects all records for detached houses. Include all fields. Save the query as *Detached*.

2   Create a mailing label report like the one in FIGURE 23.3 to include the records in the query dynaset and the following fields:

Address

Town

3   Include the text *The Occupier* at the top of each record.

4   Save the report as *Detached*.

The Occupier
187, Dairyground Road
Chelmer

The Occupier
258, Chelmer Lane
Meriton

The Occupier
4, The Crescent
Branford

The Occupier
66, Dairyground Road
Chelmer

The Occupier
14, Holly Road
Branford

The Occupier
Oaklands, The Crescent
Branford

FIGURE 23.3 Mailing label report

Task 4: Customising a report

This task involves additional customisation of the **Properties** report created in
Task 1. The objective is to produce a report that looks similar to that in FIGURE
23.4.

1   Open the **Properties** report.

2   Move and size the controls on the **Properties** report so that they are positioned
    as in FIGURE 23.4.

3   Modify the size of the report areas so that they just accommodate the appropri-
    ate text.

4   Modify the font of appropriate controls, by changing their size and style (e.g.
    bold or italic) to match more closely those in FIGURE 23.4.

5   Add lines and rectangles to the report as indicated in FIGURE 23.4.

6   Add borders to controls as indicated in FIGURE 23.4.

Properties

Selling Price	£35,000.00	Property No	10
Address 34, Adelaide Road		**Date of Entry**	
Town Chelmer		02 January 1996	

Selling Price	£39,000.00	Property No	20
Address Flat 4, 346, Chelmer Lane		**Date of Entry**	
Town Chelmer		29 June 1996	

Selling Price	£45,000.00	Property No	18
Address Flat 1, Gracelands		**Date of Entry**	
Town Woodford		20 June 1996	

FIGURE 23.4 Customised Properties report

Relational databases

What you will learn in this unit

All the units so far have considered forms, queries and reports that are ultimately based on one table. A relational database management system, such as Access, allows more than one table to be created in a database and enables you to establish links between these tables, using common fields. This unit provides a brief introduction to the concept of a relational database and considers the advantages of storing data in separate files.

To explore how the Chelmer Leisure database can be developed into a relational database you should move on to *Access 97 Further Skills*.

Understanding relationships between tables

We have created two databases, one concerning a leisure centre and the other an estate agency. Each database has one basic table, although a second table (Classes) has been included in the leisure centre database. However, if we were to consider all these businesses' functions then there may be much more data concerning different areas of the business that could be stored in the database. This is not an easy job in real life and is usually performed by systems analysts, who are trained in designing database systems to meet the needs of specific businesses.

Chelmer Leisure and Recreation Centre is one such business, although its operation and the information flows that these generate are much less complex than might be encountered in larger multi-national business.

A leisure centre basically needs a building, staff and customers. Often it is cheaper to take out membership of a leisure centre than pay each time you go, and some centres require you to become a member before you can use their facilities. When someone joins the centre, details about that person, such as name and address, are obtained. Details about the staff who work at the centre will also be needed so that they can be paid correctly, e.g. name, salary and national insurance number. Details about room, halls and courts bookings will be needed so that the building is used efficiently. Staff then know which facilities are being used and when, allowing for activity and room scheduling. In respect of the centre's bar or café inventory, details about stocks of food and drink would need to be kept as well as, for example, sales records.

Let's begin by reviewing membership data in more detail. What sort of information will the centre be asking for in the membership form? Apart from name and address, date of birth is useful for targeting advertising to specific groups, e.g. senior citizens, and knowing about members' sporting interests is also useful.

The information that Chelmer Leisure and Recreation Centre requires about each new member is shown in the following table:

Lastname	Occupation
Firstname	Date of Birth
Title	Date of Joining
Street	Date of Last Renewal
Town	Sporting Interests
County	Smoker
Post Code	Sex
Telephone No	

The table contents are the names of each piece or field of information. Before issuing a membership card the centre will allocate a unique membership number, and will charge a membership fee. It offers different categories of membership for which different fees are charged.

The centre will need to hold data about the current fees charged for each category of membership. This would form another table in our system, the membership category table, which would have the following fields:

Category No
Category Type
Membership Fee

To discover the fee that a member has paid by matching his or her membership category with Category No in the membership category table (above), the information in the two tables can be linked. This is known as relating the tables, and by creating links between them, they appear to be one table.

One advantage of using more than one table is that less storage space is required. Consider the situation where there wasn't a membership category table and the information about category type and membership fee was stored in the table containing the member's information. If there are, say, 500 members, 500 membership category descriptions and 500 membership fee details must to be stored. However, with two tables there will be 500 category identification numbers in the main table, which need only be one digit, and if there are six categories, the second table will contain six category identification numbers, six descriptions and six fee details. Another advantage is that the fees can be amended and the new data is available throughout the database simultaneously, so that when a new member joins or membership is renewed the correct fee details are used. Since the membership and membership categories are related through the **Category No** field it is possible to create printouts (reports) that include data from both tables.

We have already considered and created a table that can hold data concerning classes being held by the centre. Another table that could form part of the Chelmer Leisure and Recreation Centre system might refer to bookings of the rooms, halls and courts. The centre will need to keep track of room bookings to prevent double booking and to schedule classes. Rooms can be booked either by members or by a class so there is one link between a member and a room booking, and another between a class and a room booking. The Bookings and Classes tables are shown below.

Bookings table	Classes table
Booking No	Class No
Room/Hall/Court	Class Day
Member/Class	Class Time
Member No	Class Tutor
Class No	Class Activity
Date	Male/Female/Mixed
Time	

FIGURE 24.1, which shows the relational database that could be used by a system for Chelmer Leisure and Recreation Centre, is the one used in *Access 97 Further Skills*. It shows how the four tables: Membership, Membership Category, Classes and Bookings are linked through common fields.

This is just one database structure that could be used for part of the system at Chelmer Leisure and Recreation Centre. The total system would be more complex and a number of alternative database structures are possible. The best structure for a given application depends on the way in which the database is to be used or, more specifically, what information customers and managers need to be able to extract from it.

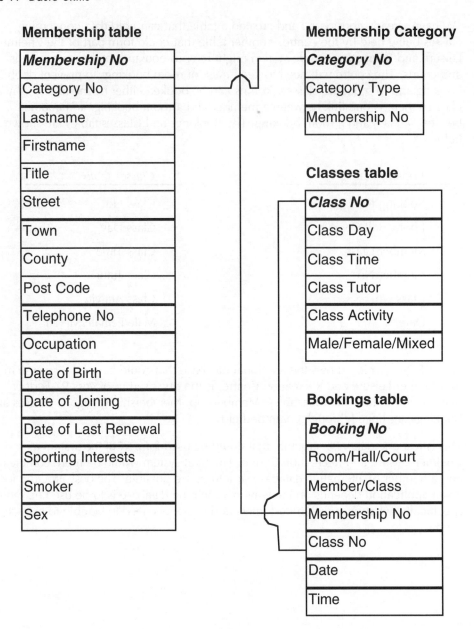

Membership table

| Membership No |
| Category No |
| Lastname |
| Firstname |
| Title |
| Street |
| Town |
| County |
| Post Code |
| Telephone No |
| Occupation |
| Date of Birth |
| Date of Joining |
| Date of Last Renewal |
| Sporting Interests |
| Smoker |
| Sex |

Membership Category

| Category No |
| Category Type |
| Membership No |

Classes table

| Class No |
| Class Day |
| Class Time |
| Class Tutor |
| Class Activity |
| Male/Female/Mixed |

Bookings table

| Booking No |
| Room/Hall/Court |
| Member/Class |
| Membership No |
| Class No |
| Date |
| Time |

FIGURE 24.1 Chelmer Leisure and Recreation Centre Database

Task 1: Creating and linking tables

The Centre will need to have details of the class tutors that it employs. Design a **Tutors** table on paper by considering the fields that will comprise the records in this table. How could this table be linked in with the tables in FIGURE 24.1?

Creating queries and reports based on more than one table

By defining a relationship between two or more tables, the tables can appear to act as one table, and you can generate queries and reports from them. Creating a very simple relationship using the estate agency database will be considered in the following task.

Task 2: Creating a query and report based on linked tables

In this task you will create a table that lists the descriptions of house types and link it to the main table. You will then create query and report based on the two tables.

1   Open the Chelmer Estates database.

2   Create a table which lists the types of properties as illustrated below (see step 3).

1	bungalow
2	detached
3	semi-detached
4	terraced
5	flat

3   Define the two fields, **House Type** (Number - Double) and **Description** (Text - 50). Save the table as **Property Type** without setting a primary key. Enter the data shown above and close the table.

4   Create a new query in design view and add both tables. Click on the **House Type** field in the **Properties** table and drag it to the **House Type** field in the **Property Type** table. Access will draw a line between the two tables, indicating a link.

5   Add to the query the fields **Address** and **Town** from the **Properties** table, **Description** from the **Property Type** table, and **Selling Price** from the **Properties** table. Set a criterion to select properties below £75,000. View the query and save it as **Lower Priced Properties**. Create a report based on this query.

Summary

The aim of these units has been to introduce you to the basics of Access 97, in terms of how to create a simple database and how to organise, select and print the data held within it. Using database management software is perhaps not as easy to get to grips with as other types of software such as wordprocessors or spreadsheets, mainly because of the different components making up the database and the additional planning required to set it up. However, we hope you have enjoyed using Access which, because of its user-friendly interface, makes it easier to learn. You will have noted from time to time references to the *Access 97 Further Skills* text, which we strongly recommend you use to learn more about using Access.

Quick reference: Data for tables

Membership table data

Note that the membership number cannot be entered directly, Access will allocate it. If you delete a record you will lose that number but this does not matter, so if your membership numbers are different don't worry - just make a note of the differences for reference when you are working on a task that uses the membership number.

Membership no	Category	Lastname	Firstname	Title	Street
1	2	Walker	Andrew J	Mr	16 Dovecot Close
2	1	Cartwright	Denise	Mrs	27 Bowling Green Rd
3	6	Perry	Jason R	Mr	59 Church Street
4	2	Forsythe	Ann M	Miss	2 Ferndale Close
5	1	Jameson	Donna	Mrs	25 Alder Drive
6	3	Robinson	Petra	Miss	16 Lowton Lane
7	5	Harris	David J	Mr	55 Coven Road
8	2	Shangali	Imran	Mr	47 High Street
9	1	Barrett	Martha A	Mrs	7 Oldcott Way
10	1	Weiner	George W F	Mr	6 Church Street
11	6	Ali	David	Mr	33 Meirton Road
12	2	Young	Aileen	Ms	78 Highgate Street
13	5	Gray	Ivor P	Mr	4 The Parade
14	5	Swift	Freda	Miss	23 Ferndale Close
15	1	Davies	Sandra M	Mrs	61 Hallfield Road
16	1	Robinson	Rebecca	Mrs	9 Moss Street
17	2	Everett	Alan	Mr	12 Stanley Street
18	4	Locker	Liam	Mr	2 Beech Close
19	4	Locker	Alison	Miss	2 Beech Close
20	1	Jones	Edward R	Mr	17 Mayfield Avenue

	Town	County	Post code	Telephone no	Occupation	Date of birth
1	Chelmer	Cheshire	CH2 6TR	01777 569236	Builder	12/3/52
2	Meriton	Cheshire	CH9 2EV	01777 552099	Housewife	29/11/60
3	Chelmer	Cheshire	CH1 8YU			3/6/82
4	Chelmer	Cheshire		01777 569945	Receptionist	5/8/73
5	Chelmer	Cheshire	CH2 7FN		Housewife	4/12/70
6	Branford	Staffs	ST10 2DZ	01778 890523		7/7/84
7	Chelmer	Cheshire	CH3 8PS	01777 569311	Retired	22/5/28
8	Chelmer	Cheshire	CH1 7JH	01777 561553	Accountant	15/3/55
9	Meriton	Cheshire	CH9 3DR	01777 557822	Teacher	25/11/60
10	Chelmer	Cheshire	CH1 8YV		Electrician	10/2/58

11	Chelmer	Cheshire	CH4 5KD	01777 569066		14/7/81
12	Branford	Staffs	ST10 4RT	01778 894471	Civil Servant	25/10/51
13	Chelmer	Cheshire	CH1 7ER	01777 565715	Unemployed	12/4/47
14	Chelmer	Cheshire	CH2 8PN	01777 567351	Retired	14/9/27
15	Meriton	Cheshire	CH9 1YJ	01778 891441	Clerk	1/2/65
16	Chelmer	Cheshire	CH2 8SE	01777 568812	Housewife	18/5/68
17	Chelmer	Cheshire	CH3 3CJ		Draughtsperson	30/7/57
18	Chelmer	Cheshire	CH3 8UH			30/12/83
19	Chelmer	Cheshire	CH3 8UH			30/12/83
20	Chelmer	Cheshire	CH2 9OL	01777 567333	Bus Driver	22/12/58

	Date of joining	*Date of last renewal*	*Sporting interests*	*Smoker*	*Sex*
1	3/2/92	3/2/97	Tennis, squash	Yes	Yes
2	16/7/91	16/7/96	Aerobics, swimming, running, squash	No	No
3	12/12/96	12/12/96	Judo, Karate	No	Yes
4	16/9/91	16/9/96		No	No
5	15/6/93	15/6/96	Aerobics, squash	Yes	No
6	3/1/95	3/1/97	Swimming, Judo	No	No
7	1/2/94	1/2/97	Badminton, cricket	Yes	Yes
8	6/4/92	6/4/96	Weight training, squash	No	Yes
9	4/10/93	4/10/96	Keep fit, swimming	No	No
10	15/7/92	15/7/96	Weight training, squash	No	Yes
11	2/10/94	2/10/96	Judo, swimming, football	No	Yes
12	9/8/92	9/8/96	Keep fit, Aerobics, squash	Yes	No
13	5/1/97	5/1/97		Yes	Yes
14	16/9/93	16/9/96		No	No
15	5/4/92	5/4/97	Aerobics, squash, swimming	Yes	No
16	6/12/91	6/12/96	Tennis, Aerobics	No	No
17	5/11/93	5/11/96	Squash, Fitness training, football	No	Yes
18	13/6/92	13/6/97		No	Yes
19	13/6/92	13/6/97		No	No
20	17/5/91	17/5/96	Weight training	Yes	Yes

Classes table data

Class no	Class day	Class time	Class tutor	Class activity	Male/female/ mixed
1	Monday	10:00	Evans	Ladies' Aerobics	Female
2	Monday	11:00	Franks	Weight Training	Male
3	Monday	15:00	Latham	Body Conditioning	Mixed
4	Monday	19:00	Wheildon	Step Aerobics	Mixed
5	Tuesday	10:00	Jackson	Men's Multi-gym	Male
6	Tuesday	14:00	Adams	Ladies' Multi-gym	Female
7	Tuesday	19:00	Jackson	Family Multi-gym	Mixed

8	Wednesday	10:00	Evans	Ladies' Aerobics	Female
9	Wednesday	14:00	Latham	Body Conditioning	Mixed
10	Wednesday	15:00	Franks	Weight Training	Female
11	Wednesday	19:00	Franks	Weight Training	Mixed
12	Thursday	11:00	Latham	Weight Training	Male
13	Thursday	14:00	Wheildon	Step Aerobics	Mixed
14	Thursday	15:00	Adams	Multi-gym	Mixed
15	Thursday	19:00	Latham	Body Conditioning	Mixed
16	Friday	10:00	Latham	Body Conditioning	Female
17	Friday	11:00	Wheildon	Step Aerobics	Mixed
18	Friday	14:00	Jackson	Men's Multi-gym	Male

Estate Agency data - Properties table

Note that the property number cannot be entered directly, Access will allocate it. If you delete a record you will lose that number but this does not matter, so if your property numbers are different don't worry. They are listed sequentially here but you will notice that they are different in the tasks as records were deleted in our sample database.

Property no	Address	Town	House type	Number of bedrooms	Garage	Garden length
1	3, Bude Close	Chelmer	3	4	1	40
2	56, Bodmin Drive	Chelmer	3	3	1	30
3	187, Dairyground Road	Chelmer	2	4	2	80
4	2, Woodford Road	Meriton	4	2	3	100
5	16, The Close	Branford	3	3	1	50
6	67, Seal Road	Chelmer	3	5	1	75
7	258, Chelmer Lane	Meriton	2	3	1	120
8	34, Adelaide Road	Chelmer	5	1	1	0
9	345, Chelmer Lane	Chelmer	3 .	6	1	200
10	16, Park Road	Chelmer	1	4	2	250
11	4, The Crescent	Branford	2	6	2	300
12	66, Dairyground Road	Chelmer	2	4	2	90
13	15, Pownall Lane	Chelmer	1	3	1	50
14	158, Moss Lane	Chelmer	1	2	1	60
15	34, The Grove	Chelmer	4	3	0	40
16	Flat 1, Gracelands	Woodford	5	2	0	0
17	14, Holly Road	Branford	2	7	2	500
18	Flat 4, 346, Chelmer Lane	Chelmer	5	1	1	0
19	4, St Paul's Avenue	Chelmer	3	3	1	70
20	Oaklands, The Crescent	Branford	2	5	2	150
21	18, Merrylands	Branford	2	6	2	100

	Leasehold/ freehold	Selling price	Heating	Date of entry	Notes
1	Leasehold	100000	1	12 June 1995	granny flat, listed, double glazing
2	Freehold	50000	2	20 September 1995	triangular garden, integral garage, double glazing
3	Freehold	111000	2	01 October 1995	cloakroom
4	Freehold	55000	0	21 October 1995	listed
5	Leasehold	45000	1	18 November 1995	
6	Leasehold	87000	3	04 December 1995	extended accommodation, in need of renovation
7	Freehold	89000	1	15 December 1995	listed thatched cottage, thoroughly renovated and modernised
8	Leasehold	35000	2	02 January 1996	
9	Freehold	150000	4	05 January 1996	
10	Freehold	200000	1	05 January 1996	luxury home, cloak room
11	Freehold	300000	1	10 January 1996	luxury home, granny flat, cloakroom
12	Freehold	115000	2	12 January 1996	granny flat
13	Freehold	80000	1	04 April 1996	
14	Freehold	60000	2	03 May 1996	
15	Leasehold	65000	0	21 May 1996	in need of some additional renovation, listed
16	Freehold	45000	3	20 June 1996	
17	Freehold	400000	4	21 June 1996	rural property with land, granny flat, cloakroom
18	Leasehold	39000	2	29 June 1996	
19	Freehold	67000	1	04 July 1996	
20	Freehold	250000	1	15 August 1996	
21	Freehold	120000	1	09 September 1996	

Data definitions

Classes table

Columns

Name		Type	Size
Class No	*Index*: Primary key	AutoNumber	4
Class Day	*Required*: True	Text	10
Class Time	*Format*: hh:mm Short time	Date/Time	8
Class Tutor		Text	30
Class Activity	*Required*: True	Text	20
Male/Female/ Mixed	*Validation Rule*: "Male" or "Female" or "Mixed" *Validation Text*: Please enter Male, Female or Mixed	Text	10

Membership table

Columns

Name		Type	Size
Membership No	*Description*: Automatic membership numbering *Index*: Primary key	Number (Long)	4
Category No	*Description*: Categories are 1-Senior, 2-Senior Club, 3-Junior, 4-Junior Club, 5-Concessionary, 6-Youth Club *Validation Rule*: <=6 *Validation Text*: Please enter a category between 1 and 6 *Required*: True	Number (Byte)	1
Lastname	*Required*: True	Text	25
Firstname		Text	30
Title		Text	10
Street	*Required*: True	Text	30
Town	*Default value*: Chelmer *Required*: True	Text	25
County	*Default value*: Cheshire *Required*: True	Text	20
Post Code	*Format:*>	Text	10
Telephone No		Text	12
Occupation		Text	50
Date of Birth	*Format*: short date	Date/Time	8
Date of Joining	*Format*: short date	Date/Time	8
Date of Last Renewal	*Format*: short date	Date/Time	8
Sporting Interests		Memo	0
Smoker	*Format*: ;"Smoker"; "Non-Smoker"	Yes/No	1
Sex	*Format*: ;"Male";"Female"	Yes/No	1

Properties table

Columns

Name		Type	Size
Property No	*Description*: automatic registration numbering	Number (Long)	4
Address	*Description*: number, street name	Text	30
Town	*Default value*: Chelmer	Text	25
House Type	*Description*: 1= bungalow, 2= detached, 3=semi-detached, 4= terraced, 5= flat *Validation Rule*: <=5 *Validation Text*: Please enter a category number between 1 and 5	Number (Double)	8
Number of Bedrooms		Number (Double)	8
Garage	*Description*: 1= single, 2= double, 3= none *Validation Rule*: <=3 *Validation Text*: Please enter a category number between 1 and 3	Number (Double)	8
Garden Length		Number (Double)	8
Leasehold/ Freehold	*Format*: ;"Leasehold"; "Freehold"	Yes/No	1
Selling Price		Number (Double)	8
Heating	*Description*: 1=gas, 2 = electric, 3= solid fuel, 4 = oil *Validation Rule*: <=4 *Validation Text*: Please enter a category number between 1 and 4	Number (Double)	8
Date of Entry		Date/Time (Long Date)	8
Notes		Memo	

Quick reference: Basic Windows operations and Access toolbars

Some readers will not be familiar with Windows, and Access may well be one of the first Windows products encountered by these users. Any reader who has not previously used Windows is strongly recommended to run through the Windows tutorial which introduces users to mouse techniques and the basic operation of Windows. This tutorial can be found by clicking on **Start**, selecting **Help**, clicking on the **Contents** tab, selecting **Introducing Windows**, clicking on **Open** and selecting **Tour: Ten minutes to using Windows**. This unit briefly summarises some of the key operations and should act as a ready reference to some of the terminology that is used elsewhere in the book.

Mouse pointer shapes

When you point the mouse to different parts of the screen, the pointer shape changes, allowing you to perform different tasks. Some commands also change the pointer shape.

The table below lists some common pointer shapes as encountered in Access.

Pointer shape	*Meaning*
I	The pointer which appears over the text area. Click to position an insertion point where text may be typed.
 �	The pointer appears over menus, non-text areas of windows, inactive windows, scroll bars, or toolbars. You can choose a menu and command or click a toolbar button. You can also use this pointer to drag to make a selection.
 ☝	The pointer is over the selection bar, for example, at the edge of a table, or at the left edge of a cell. You can select a cell, a row, or several rows.
⌛	Access is performing a task that will take a few seconds.
 ‡ ╬	Appear along the borders between window sections or columns. Drag to resize the section or column.
 �?	This pointer appears after you press *Shift-F1*. You can point to any item on the screen and click to view specific Help.
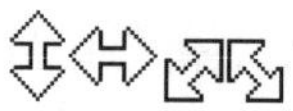 ⇳⇔⤢⤡	The pointer is on a window border. The pointer will assume one of the shapes opposite, depending on which part of the border. Drag to resize the window.
 ✛	This pointer appears when you have selected the **Move** or **Size** command from the **Control** menu. You can move the window to a new position or drag the window border.
↓	This pointer appears over the grey bar at the top of a column in a table, query, or filter. Click to select the column.
→	This pointer appears in the record selection bar. Click to select record.
 �	This is the drag and drop pointer, which appears when you make a selection and drag the selection to its new location. Release the mouse button to drop or insert the selection.
Q	This is the zoom pointer which appears in print preview.
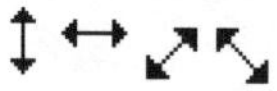 ↕ ↔ ↙ ↘	The pointer is on a control sizing handle. Depending on which handle you select, the pointer will assume one of the shapes opposite. Drag to resize the control.
 ☝	In form or report design this pointer is used to move an individual label or control.
✋	In form or report design this pointer is used to move a label and control or a selected set of controls.
✛	This pointer appears with a Toolbox icon and indicates the position of the control on the form or report design. Click to position the control.

Basics of Windows: a quick review

The Windows screen has the following features.

Menu bar

The Menu bar shows the titles of the various pull down menus that are available within a given application. To select a menu option, first select the menu by placing the mouse pointer over the name of the menu on the Menu bar and click the left mouse button. The menu will appear. Move the mouse pointer to the menu option you require and click the left mouse button again. Note that any menu options displayed in light grey are not currently available. Menus can also be accessed via the keyboard. For example, to select the file menu press *Alt+F* i.e. press *Alt* together with the initial letter of the menu option.

Control menu

The **Control** menu is found on all windows whether they be application windows or document windows. To access the **Control** menu click on the **Control Menu** box in the upper left corner of the window, or press *Alt+Spacebar*. The exact contents are different for different windows, but typically basic windows operations such as restore, move, size, minimise, maximise, and close are represented.

Title bar

The Title bar tells you which window is displayed. By pointing the mouse at the window's Title bar and then dragging it to a new location the window can removed.

Task bar

At the bottom of your screen is the Task bar. It contains the **Start** button, which you can use to start a program quickly or to find a file. It's also the fastest way to get help.

When you open a program, document, or window, a button appears on the Task bar. You can use this button to switch between open windows quickly.

Maximize, Minimize and Restore buttons

Clicking on the **Maximize** button enlarges a window to its maximum size, so that it fills the whole desktop.

Clicking on the **Restore** button will restore a maximised window to its previous size.

Clicking on the **Mimimize** button reduces the window to a small icon at the bottom of the screen. When you shrink an application window to an icon, the application is still running in memory, but its window is not taking up space on your desktop.

Clicking on the **Close** button closes the window.

Dialog boxes

Windows uses dialog boxes to request information from you and to provide information to you. Most dialog boxes include options, with each option asking for a different kind of information.

After all the requested information has been supplied you choose a command button to carry out the command. Two that feature on every dialog box are **OK** and **Cancel**. **OK** causes the command to be executed. **Cancel** cancels the operation and removes the dialog box from the screen. These buttons represent the two means of quitting from a dialog box. To choose a command button, click on it or if the button is currently active, press *ENTER*.

There are a number of types of dialog boxes.

- *Text boxes* are boxes where you are allowed to type in text, such as a filename. The presence of a flashing vertical bar, or the insertion point, indicates that the text box is active and that you may enter text. If the text box is not active, place the mouse pointer on the box and click. The insertion point will then appear in the box.

- *List boxes* display a column of available choices. Items can be selected from a list box by double clicking on the item, or clicking once on the item and then clicking on the **OK** button.

- *Check boxes* offer a list of options that you can switch on and off. You can select as many or as few check box options as are applicable. When an option in a check box is selected it contains a ✓; otherwise the box is empty. To select a check box, click on the empty box.

- *Option buttons* appear as a list of mutually exclusive items. You can select only one option from the list at a time. You can change a selection by selecting a different button. The selected button contains a black dot. To select an option button, click on it.

- *Scroll bars* appear at the side of windows and list boxes. They appear when the information contained in a window cannot all be displayed within that window. Both vertical and horizontal scroll bars may be present, depending on whether the database object is too long or too wide to fit on the screen. The small box in the middle of the bar represents the position of the currently displayed screen within the whole object. You can move to a different position in the object by moving this box. You can move this box either by clicking on the scroll bar arrow boxes, clicking on the scroll bar itself, or dragging the box.

Access toolbar buttons

Database window

Button	Function
New Database	Creates a new database
Open Database	Opens an existing database
Save	Saves database
Print	Print definition of highlighted object
Print Preview	Previews the object definition
Spelling	Runs the spell checker
Cut	Removes selection to the clipboard
Copy	Copies selection to the clipboard
Paste	Pastes the contents of clipboard to current position
Format Painter	Copies formatting
Undo	Undoes the last action
OfficeLinks	Exports to MS Word mail merge, document or MS Excel
Analyze	Analyses table, analyses performance, invokes Documenter
Large Icons	Lists database objects in large icons for the selected object type
Small Icons	Lists database objects in small icons for the selected object type
List	Lists icons alphabetically
Details	Lists icon details, e.g. size and creation date
Code	Displays a Visual Basic module window
Properties	Displays the general properties of the currently selected object
Relationships	Displays the Relationships window
New Object	Creates a new table, query, form, report, macro or zmodule, or launches AutoForm or AutoReport
Office Assistant	Invokes the Office Assistant

Table Design View

Button	Function
(Table) View	Displays the data in the table in the form of a datasheet
Save	Saves the table
Print	Print
Print Preview	Print Preview
Spelling	Spell check
Cut	Removes selection to the clipboard
Copy	Copies selection to the clipboard
Paste	Pastes the contents of clipboard to current position
Format Painter	Copies formatting
Undo	Undoes the last action
Primary Key	Sets primary key for selected field(s)
Indexes	Displays the Indexes dialog box
Insert Rows	Inserts row(s)
Delete Rows	Deletes row(s)
Properties	Display properties of table
Build	Displays a builder for the selected item or property (only enabled if builder available)
Database Window	Displays the Database window
New Object	Creates a new table, query, form, report, macro or module, or launches AutoForm or AutoReport
Office Assistant	Invokes the Office Assistant

Query Design View

Button	Function
(Query) View	Displays the data in the query in the form of a datasheet
Save	Saves the query
Print	Prints the active object
Print Preview	Print previews the active object
Spelling	Spell checks
Cut	Removes selection to the clipboard
Copy	Copies selection to the clipboard
Paste	Pastes the contents of clipboard to current position
Format Painter	Copies formatting
Undo	Undoes the last action
Query Type	Drop down list for choice of Select query (default), Crosstab query (for summarising data), Make Table query, Update query, Append query or Delete query
Run	Runs the query
Show Table	Displays the Show Table dialog box for adding tables
Totals	Displays total row in QBE (query by example) grid for statistical summary
Top Values	Finds the top values in the active query based on a percentage or number of rows
Properties	Displays the properties of the query
Build	Displays the Expression builder
Database Window	Displays the Database window
New Object	Creates a new table, query, form, report, macro or module, or launches AutoForm or AutoReport
Office Assistant	Invokes the Office Assistant

Datasheet and Form View

Button	Function
(Table) View	Displays table design
Save	Saves the table layout
Print	Prints the datasheet
Print Preview	Displays the print preview
Spelling	Spell check
Cut	Removes selection to clipboard
Copy	Copies selection to clipboard
Paste	Pastes from clipboard to current position
Format Painter	Copies formatting
Undo	Undoes the last action
Insert Hyperlink	Inserts or modifies a hyperlink address
Web Toolbar	Displays or hides the Web toolbar
Sort Ascending	Displays records in ascending order of current field
Sort Descending	Displays records in descending order of current field
Filter By Selection	Filters records based on selected data
Filter By Form	Displays a form for the entry of filter criteria
Apply Filter	Displays filtered records
Find	Searches for selected data
New Record	Goes to new record
Delete Record	Removes record
Database Window	Displays the Database window
New Object	Creates a new table, query, form, report, macro or module, or launches AutoForm or AutoReport
Office Assistant	Invokes the Office Assistant

Form Design View

Button	Function
(Form) View	Runs the form
Save	Saves the form
Print	Prints the form
Print Preview	Displays the print preview
Spelling	Spell checks
Cut	Removes selection to clipboard
Copy	Copies selection to clipboard
Paste	Pastes from clipboard to current position
Format Painter	Copies formatting from one control to another. Double-click to copy to several controls, *Esc* to finish
Undo	Undoes the last action
Insert Hyperlink	Inserts or modifies a hyperlink address
Web Toolbar	Displays or hides the Web toolbar
Field List	Displays the Field List window
Toolbox	Displays the Toolbox window
AutoFormat	Applies your choice of predefined formats to the form
Code	Displays an Access Basic form module in the Module window
Properties	Displays the properties sheet
Build	Displays a builder for the selected item or property (only enabled if builder available)
Database Window	Displays Database window
New Object	Creates a new table, query, form, report, macro or module, or launches AutoForm or AutoReport
Office Assistant	Invokes the Office Assistant
Object	Selects entire form, section of a form or a control
Font	Displays list of font names
Font Size	Displays list of font sizes
Bold	Applies bold typeface

Button	Function
Italic	Applies italic typeface
Underline	Applies underlining
Align Left	Left aligns contents of label or control
Center	Centre aligns contents of label or control
Align Right	Right aligns contents of label or control
Back Color	Drop down background colour selection
Fore Color	Drop down foreground colour selection
Line/Border Color	Drop down border or line colour selection
Line/Border Width	Drop down border or line width selection
Special Effect	Drop down special effect (raised, sunken etc) selection

Report Design View

Button	Function
(Report) View	Previews report
Save	Saves the report
Print	Prints the report
Print Preview	Displays a print preview
Spelling	Spell checks
Cut	Removes selection to clipboard
Copy	Copies selection to clipboard
Paste	Pastes from clipboard to current position
Format Painter	Copies formatting from one control to another. Double click to copy to several controls, *Esc* to finish
Undo	Undoes the last action
Insert Hyperlink	Inserts or modifies a hyperlink address
Web Toolbar	Displays or hides the Web toolbar
Field List	Displays the Field List window
Toolbox	Displays the Toolbox window
Sorting and Grouping	Displays the Sorting and Grouping dialog box
AutoFormat	Applies your choice of predefined formats to the report

Button	Function
Code	Displays an Access Basic report module in the Module window
Properties	Displays the properties sheet
Build	Displays a builder for the selected item or property (only enabled if builder available)
Database Window	Displays Database window
New Object	Create a new table, query, form, report, macro or module, or launch AutoForm or AutoReport
Office Assistant	Invokes the Office Assistant
Select Object	Selects entire report, section of a report or a control
Font	Displays list of font names
Font Size	Displays list of font sizes
Bold	Applies bold typeface
Italic	Applies italic typeface
Underline	Applies underlining
Align Left	Left aligns contents of label or control
Center	Centre aligns contents of label or control
Align Right	Right aligns contents of label or control
Fill/Back Color	Drop down background colour selection
Fore/Front Color	Drop down foreground colour selection
Line/Border Color	Drop down border or line colour selection
Line/Border Width	Drop down border or line width selection
Special Effect	Drop down special effect (raised, sunken etc) selection

Report and Form Print preview

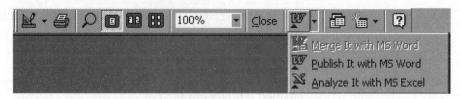

Button	Function
View	Switches to design view
Print	Prints
Zoom	Toggle to zoom in or out
One Page	Displays print preview one page format
Two Pages	Displays print preview two page format
Multiple Pages	Displays print preview in multiple page format as specified
Zoom	Controls the amount of magnification
Close	Closes preview and returns to design
Merge It with MS Word	Saves the output of a table, query, form, report or module to a file, and then attaches the file to a message in your electronic mail program
Publish It with MS Word	Saves the output of a datasheet, query, form or report to a file in Rich Text Format (RTF), suitable for importing into Word or other Windows wordprocessors or desktop publishing applications
Analyze It with MS Excel	Saves the output of a datasheet, query, form, or report, to a file in Microsoft Excel (.XLS) format.
Database Window	Displays the Database window
New Object	Creates a new table, query, form, report, macro or module, or launch AutoForm or AutoReport
Office Assistant	Invokes the Office Assistant

Glossary

Access	A relational database product.
Alignment	Whether the characters in a control start at the left side of the control, end at the right side of the control or are centred on the control's position.
Case sensitive	Distinguishing between upper and lower case text.
Check boxes	Boxes offering a list of options which you can switch on or off.
Click	Position the pointer and quickly press and release the left mouse button.
Control	Individual design element.
Control menu	The menu found on all windows accessed by clicking on the Control Menu box in the upper left corner of the window.
Data type	The type of data allowed in a particular field.
Database	A collection of related data.
DataBase Management System (DBMS)	Software used to present data stored in a computer.
Database window	The first window presented after creating or opening a database.
Datasheet View	The view from which you can enter data in tables.
Default value	A value entered in a field automatically by Access.
Design View	The view from which you can design tables, forms, reports and queries.
Detail	The detail of a report, that is, the data from records in a database.
Dialog box	A box used to request information or to provide information.
Double click	Position the pointer and quickly press and release the left mouse button twice.
Drag	Position the pointer. Press and hold down the left mouse button as you move the mouse to the desired position and then release the button.
Dynaset	The result of a query.
Field	A piece of data within a record.
Field description	The description of a field. It may be up to 255 characters long.
Field list	A list of fields that a form was based upon.
Field name	The name of a field. Field names can be up to 64 characters including spaces. Full stops (.), exclamation marks (!) and square brackets ([ ]) are not allowed.
Field properties	Detailed definitions of a data type.
Filter	A means of displaying selected records.

Font	A collection of features that describes how text appears.
Form	An on-screen method of collecting information for a database.
Group footer	Text marking the end of a group in a report.
Group header	Text marking the beginning of a group in a report.
Grouped report	A report with selected fields placed in a row. Records are grouped according to the value of a field in the table or query.
List boxes	Boxes showing a column of available choices.
Mailing label reports	Reports for creating mailing labels.
Maximize button	The button that enlarges a window to its maximum size.
Menu bar	The bar showing titles of various pull down menus that are available in an application.
Minimize button	The button that reduces a window to a small icon at the bottom of the screen.
Null value	An empty field.
Option buttons	A list of mutually exclusive items.
Page footer	Text that appears at the bottom of every page of a report.
Page header	Text which appears at the top of each page of a report such as a running title and page number.
Point	Position the mouse pointer on or next to something.
Preview	A miniature version of what is to be printed, displayed on the screen.
Primary key	A field or combination of fields that uniquely identifies a record.
Properties sheet	A list of properties.
Queries	A method of asking questions of a database.
Query criteria	The method of framing questions to allow specific records to be retrieved from the database.
Query Design window	The window from which you design a query.
Record	A set of details about an individual item. Each item has a separate record in the table.
Report footer	Information at the end of a report.
Report header	The heading and introductory text at the beginning of a report.
Report	Collection of information suitable for printing.
Restore button	The button that restores a maximised window to its previous size.
Row selector symbols	Symbols at the edge of a table row, which enable you to select a row of information.
Screen forms	The method of customising the way in which the data from records in table or queries are displayed on the screen.

Scroll bars	Bars which appear at the side of windows and list boxes when all the information cannot be displayed within the window. They allow you to scroll through the information.
Single column form	A form which allows the user to input one record at a time.
Single column report	A report with all selected fields in a single column.
String	A collection of characters (letters, numbers, and punctuation marks) that make up the data in a field.
Table Design window	The interface that allows you to define the structure of your table.
Tables	The method by which Access stores data.
Tabular form	A form which displays more than one record on the screen.
Task bar	The bar at the bottom of the screen containing the Start button.
Text boxes	Boxes which allow you to type text.
Title bar	Top section of a window containing the name of the window. Changes colour to indicate whether active or inactive.
Toolbox	A selection of tools by which controls and text may be added to a form.
Validation rules	Tests used to detect mistakes in data entry.
Wizards	Simple methods of creating forms, reports, etc using preset values.